SpringerBriefs in Ethics

Springer Briefs in Ethics envisions a series of short publications in areas such as business ethics, bioethics, science and engineering ethics, food and agricultural ethics, environmental ethics, human rights and the like. The intention is to present concise summaries of cutting-edge research and practical applications across a wide spectrum.

Springer Briefs in Ethics are seen as complementing monographs and journal articles with compact volumes of 50 to 125 pages, covering a wide range of content from professional to academic. Typical topics might include:

- Timely reports on state-of-the art analytical techniques
- A bridge between new research results, as published in journal articles, and a contextual literature review
- A snapshot of a hot or emerging topic
- In-depth case studies or clinical examples
- Presentations of core concepts that students must understand in order to make independent contributions

Caitlin C. Corrigan · Simon Atuah Asakipaam ·
Jerry John Kponyo · Christoph Luetge
Editors

AI Ethics in Higher Education: Insights from Africa and Beyond

Editors
Caitlin C. Corrigan
Institute for Ethics in Artificial Intelligence
TUM School of Social Science
and Technology
Technical University of Munich
München, Germany

Simon Atuah Asakipaam
Department of Telecommunication
Engineering
Kwame Nkrumah University of Science
and Technology
Kumasi, Ghana

Jerry John Kponyo
Department of Telecommunication
Engineering
Kwame Nkrumah University of Science
and Technology
Kumasi, Ghana

Department of Electrical and Electronics
Engineering
Tamale Technical University
Tamale, Ghana

Christoph Luetge
Institute for Ethics in Artificial Intelligence
TUM School of Social Science
and Technology
Technical University Munich
München, Germany

ISSN 2211-8101   ISSN 2211-811X (electronic)
SpringerBriefs in Ethics
ISBN 978-3-031-23034-9   ISBN 978-3-031-23035-6 (eBook)
https://doi.org/10.1007/978-3-031-23035-6

© The Editor(s) (if applicable) and The Author(s) 2023. This book is an open access publication.
Open Access This book is licensed under the terms of the Creative Commons Attribution 4.0 International License (http://creativecommons.org/licenses/by/4.0/), which permits use, sharing, adaptation, distribution and reproduction in any medium or format, as long as you give appropriate credit to the original author(s) and the source, provide a link to the Creative Commons license and indicate if changes were made.

The images or other third party material in this book are included in the book's Creative Commons license, unless indicated otherwise in a credit line to the material. If material is not included in the book's Creative Commons license and your intended use is not permitted by statutory regulation or exceeds the permitted use, you will need to obtain permission directly from the copyright holder.

The use of general descriptive names, registered names, trademarks, service marks, etc. in this publication does not imply, even in the absence of a specific statement, that such names are exempt from the relevant protective laws and regulations and therefore free for general use.

The publisher, the authors, and the editors are safe to assume that the advice and information in this book are believed to be true and accurate at the date of publication. Neither the publisher nor the authors or the editors give a warranty, expressed or implied, with respect to the material contained herein or for any errors or omissions that may have been made. The publisher remains neutral with regard to jurisdictional claims in published maps and institutional affiliations.

This Springer imprint is published by the registered company Springer Nature Switzerland AG
The registered company address is: Gewerbestrasse 11, 6330 Cham, Switzerland

Contents

Introduction

The Need for AI Ethics in Higher Education 3
Abraham Kuuku Sam and Philipp Olbrich

Theoretical Underpinnings of AI Ethics in Practice

Teaching Ethics Applied to AI from a Cultural Standpoint: What
African "AI Ethics" for Africa? 13
Emmanuel R. Goffi

Practical Implications of Different Theoretical Approaches to AI
Ethics 27
Ugochi A. Okengwu

The Present: Best Practices and Challenges in AI Ethics Education

AI Ethics in Higher Education: Research Experiences from Practical
Development and Deployment of AI Systems 39
Joyce Nakatumba-Nabende, Conrad Suuna, and Engineer Bainomugisha

Challenges of Integrating AI Ethics into Higher Education Curricula
in West Africa: Nigerian Universities Narrative 57
Laeticia N. Onyejegbu

Promoting AI Ethics Through Awareness and Case Studies 67
Patrick E. McSharry

The Future: Visions for Responsible AI Developers

AI Ethics Education for Future African Leaders 87
Gadosey Pius Kwao, Deborah Dormah Kanubala, and Belona Sonna

Introduction

The Need for AI Ethics in Higher Education

Abraham Kuuku Sam and Philipp Olbrich

1 Artificial Intelligence as a Socio-Technical System

Business leaders, policymakers and technologists regularly portray Artificial Intelligence (AI) as an easy way to make sense of an increasingly complex world. Unsurprisingly, AI plays a central role in strategy papers, TED talks and speeches about the future of mobility, revolutions in healthcare, or scientific innovation (Bhardwaj 2018; Cornet et al. 2017). In this often techno-optimistic narrative, AI is harmless. By remaining largely in the abstract, it is possible to keep the misconception alive that AI is merely a technical tool, albeit a powerful one, to address a myriad of challenges from digital transformation to global inequality to climate change.

This changes drastically when AI moves from concept to application. The development of AI applications is embedded in its social structure. That means that the norms, values, knowledge, and attitudes of developers influence how the AI application is designed and how it works. They become an inherent part of the application itself and can lead to undesirable consequences due to biased data or algorithmic designs. This raises serious concerns when AI is used for hiring employees, offering loans or even in criminal proceedings and makes decisions based on biased data about gender, ethnicity or age. For example, the facial recognition software of leading US-American companies has been shown to better work for faces with white and male characteristics (Lohr 2018). Arguably quite similar to the group of people that developed the respective algorithms (Guynn 2019).

At the same time, AI is not used in a social vacuum. Instead, the applications serve a particular purpose in the real world. Keeping with the same example, if facial recognition is used in public CCTV or to identify suspects in criminal investigations it creates various problems (Chandran 2022). If the AI system actually works, it facilitates public surveillance of citizens with implications for their right to privacy,

---

A. K. Sam · P. Olbrich (✉)
Deutsche Gesellschaft für Internationale Zusammenarbeit (GIZ), Bonn, Germany
e-mail: philipp.olbrich@giz.de

© The Author(s) 2023
C. C. Corrigan et al. (eds.), *AI Ethics in Higher Education: Insights from Africa and Beyond*, SpringerBriefs in Ethics, https://doi.org/10.1007/978-3-031-23035-6_1

right to dissent and protest. In the more likely case that it does not work flawlessly all the time, individuals might be accused of crimes or other violations they are not involved in.

In the application settings, it becomes clear that AI is not merely a tool but a socio-technical system. One cannot clearly separate the technology from its social setting it is developed and used in—they are mutually dependent, they influence each other (see e.g., Acuto and Curtis 2014; Latour 2005). From this follow two important conclusions for the relevance of AI ethics: First, AI is no harmless tool that will solve problems of crime, health and climate change. The application of AI is driven by its developers, users, regulators, businesses and political decision-makers. They constitute the social context. This is where ethics come in as important guiding principles that define why, how and when an AI system such as facial recognition is used. Second, the development of AI technologies is not pre-determined but is contingent on their social context. They are the result of political and financial decisions as well as the individual developers who write the code. Consequently, it is not only the framework conditions that decide if AI is developed responsibly but also who writes the code. Essentially, then, it also becomes an ethical question if the diversity found in society is also found in the development teams of AI.

Acknowledging the socio-technical nature of AI does not mean ignoring the fact that responsible AI indeed offers a range of opportunities for human development and can help to achieve the Sustainable Development Goals (SDGs) (Vinuesa et al. 2020). For example, AI applications are trained with large datasets to automatically recognize and translate the language. Voice technologies allow people who cannot read and write very well to interact with digital technologies. In both cases, AI systems make access to information more inclusive and facilitate social, political and economic participation. In other instances, AI-powered apps can support smallholder farmers to identify plant diseases and take countermeasures early on. This does not only contribute to better yields but might also avoid the excessive use of herbicides. However, the responsible development and use of AI is the foundation to realize the opportunities it has to offer.

Overall, if AI is understood as a socio-technical system, ethics are relevant for both how AI is developed as well as how it is used. In turn, that means the world is neither doomed nor saved by the virtue of the power of Artificial Intelligence. However, policy-makers, businesses, civil society and, of course, AI developers are empowered to use AI ethically. They are empowered to use AI for good. As a result, they have a particular responsibility to promote the ethical development and use of AI.

2 From AI Ethics to Practice

In light of this responsibility, it is consequential to tackle the challenge of teaching AI ethics to upcoming AI practitioners and decision-makers in Africa and beyond. For doing so, this book analyzes the present and future states of AI ethics education in local Computer Science programs. It shares relevant best practices for in-class teaching, develops answers to ongoing organizational challenges and reflects on the practical implications of different theoretical approaches to AI ethics.

AI ethics can be described as "a set of values, principles, and techniques that employ widely accepted standards of right and wrong to guide moral conduct in the development and use of AI technologies" (Leslie 2019, p. 3). In this sense, the merit of AI ethics is twofold in that they encourage developers to harness the power of AI to effect positive change while it also helps them to navigate the risks (Chaturvedi et al. 2021).

At first, much of the global debate on AI ethics has remained rather abstract and high-level. In May 2019, the member countries of the Organization for Economic Cooperation and Development (OECD) adopted the so-called OECD Principles on Artificial Intelligence (OECD 2019). This counts among the first international agreements on the topic and commit signatories to ensure that AI serves the people and the planet and that it needs to respect the rule of law, human rights and democratic values. At the same time, the principles remain rather general which leaves room for interpretation on principles such as transparency of AI systems, accountability, security and safety. The vagueness and non-binding nature of the OECD principles have made them quite compatible, too, so that various non-OECD members have endorsed them as well as the G20 (OECD 2019; G20 2019). The United Nations Educational, Scientific and Cultural Organization (UNESCO) has concluded a global and more inclusive approach to AI ethics. In November 2021, the General Conference of UNESCO adopted the Recommendation on the Ethics of Artificial Intelligence (UNESCO 2021). It is the first globally accepted instrument that formulates joint values and principles. On top of that, the Recommendation defines policy actions that make suggestions on how to implement the agreed-upon values. This more action-oriented approach can also be found in the AI for Africa Blueprint that was developed by the Smart Africa Alliance under the leadership of the South African Government (Smart Africa 2021; N.B. the FAIR Forward project was involved in the development of the blueprint). The blueprint is the result of a multi-stakeholder process involving governments, the private sector and civil society. Among other things, it outlines concrete recommendations on how to create policies for responsible AI development across Africa. In early 2022, the OECD also followed up on their AI Principles and released a framework for classifying AI systems that should enable policy-makers to assess the opportunities and risks of AI applications (OECD 2022).

In doing so, the UNESCO Recommendation, the OECD framework and the Smart Africa AI Blueprint have already shown the way that AI ethics only become influential in action, i.e. when they are implemented. The question then is how to translate AI ethics into practice so that values and rights such as privacy, fairness and security are already part of the development process. In addition to the recommendations aimed at policy-makers, there are efforts to bring AI ethics into practice that put developers at the centre. On a more general note, there are approaches such as the Principles for Digital Development that outline nine overarching guidelines on how to apply digital technologies for sustainable development (Digital Principles n.d.). For instance, it requires project teams to design with the user to develop solutions, including AI, that effectively meets user needs. Moreover, it recommends using open-source software and open data to encourage more collaboration and avoid duplication of efforts.

More specific to AI are products such as the *Handbook on Data Protection and Privacy for Developers of Artificial Intelligence (AI) in India* (Chaturvedi et al. 2021; N.B. the FAIR Forward project was involved in the development of the blueprint). The handbook is the result of multiple discussions with AI start-ups, developers and practitioners. Following the development cycle of AI from data collection to data processing to roll-out, concrete prompts to encourage the developer to think through the ethical requirements of the AI application. In doing so, the handbook turns abstract principles such as transparency into concrete questions including "[a]re you aware of the source of data used for training?" or "[i]s there a mechanism for users and beneficiaries to raise a ticket for AI decisions?" (Chaturvedi et al. 2021, p. 16). While certainly not perfect, this approach serves to reduce uncertainty about the interpretation and meaning of abstract concepts. Instead, it allows AI developers and small startups who are not backed by a legal team to focus more of their time and resources on technical innovation. Quite practically, they can go through a prepared checklist during the development process and preempt ethical problems.

Moving on, the target group of AI ethics in computer science programs at institutions of higher education changes again. It does not so much comprise of policy-makers or AI startups but it begins slightly earlier with *future* AI practitioners. In many cases, university students are the AI developers of tomorrow. One fundamental way forward is equipping future AI developers with the know-how on AI ethics at an early stage in their education. That is why this book tackles the challenge of integrating concerns related to AI ethics into higher education curriculums in Africa and beyond. For in doing so, it analyzes the present and future states of AI ethics education in African Computer Science and Engineering programs. The authors share relevant best practices and use-cases for teaching, develop answers to ongoing organizational challenges and reflect on the practical implications of different theoretical approaches to AI ethics. As such, they offer useful starting points for educators, administrators and students in the field of AI in Africa and beyond. In doing so, the book does not only raise awareness of the risks of AI but offers practical tools for how to address them in university contexts.

3 Diversity of Perspective on AI Ethics in Global Higher Education

Following this introduction, the remainder of the book is divided into three parts. The subsequent section discusses the theoretical underpinnings of AI ethics in practice. In doing so, it frames the more practice-oriented contributions by outlining conceptually different approaches to how AI ethics can be understood and taught. This is followed by three chapters on best practices and current challenges in AI ethics education. Among other things, the authors offer practice-oriented research as well as anecdotal reflections on how AI ethics are and can be taught at African universities. The book then concludes with a chapter outlining what needs to happen so that Computer Science education responsibly addresses the risks of AI while seizing the opportunities it holds for economic and social development.

In the opening chapter of the theoretical section of the book, Emmanuel R. Goffi reflects on the origins of AI ethics. Given the dominance of Western thought, especially continental philosophy, he proposes a more inclusive perspective that leads to a cross-cultural approach to AI ethics. As AI can be conceived as a socio-technical system, the local context becomes relevant in both development and application. Consequently, teachers of AI ethics should embrace the variety of cultures and thought from Africa and beyond to account for the relevance of the local context. Ugochi A. Okengwu builds on this and reinforces the relevance of including African perspectives in the formulation of global AI ethics. Putting this into practice, she reviews different ethical frameworks that are applied to AI, e.g. the OECD AI Principles, to derive suggestions for practicing AI ethics in Africa.

Joyce Nakatumba-Nabende, Conrad Suuna and Engineer Bainomugisha kick off the second part of the book on present practices and challenges in AI ethics education. They empirically describe three approaches of teaching AI ethics at African universities including full course programs, AI research labs and the project-based application of AI. Drawing on practical experience, they outline concrete recommendations for how AI ethics can be best integrated into teaching emphasizing the relevance of including local African perspectives and use cases. Why and how the process of introducing AI ethics into Computer Science curricula can be challenging is discussed by Laeticia N. Onyejegbu. Following an analysis of the institutional setup using Nigeria as a case study, she presents suggestions on how AI ethics can play a more relevant role in teaching through including it in existing benchmarking standards as well as through creating stand-alone courses. Patrick McSharry takes the reader from the intricacies of education policies into the classroom. Acknowledging the real-life impact and risks of AI solutions, he demonstrates the value of case studies in teaching AI ethics. He argues that case studies help illustrate the impact of insufficient risk awareness, the dangers of privacy risks, lack of transparency and biases in data. Instructively, McSharry shares some case studies and accompanying questions that can be used by fellow educators in teaching AI ethics.

In the final chapter, Gadosey Pius Kwao, Deborah Dormah Kanubala and Belona Sonna build on the findings of the preceding chapters including the current state of AI ethics education at African educational institutions. They conclude with a set of priority measures that should be implemented to instill a sense of responsibility in future AI practitioners. Among other things, they suggest that general ethical principles as in the UNESCO AI Recommendation are a good starting point but they need to be adapted to the respective contexts to promote responsible AI development.

4 Conclusion

Certainly, AI ethics is such a broad topic that any book would be unable to cover it exhaustively. While many concepts, approaches and perspective on AI ethics have found their way into the book, it was not possible to deep-dive into specific ethical principles such as privacy, data protection and security nor to discuss the implications of legislative frameworks and certification of AI products. Future research could, for example, examine the diverse understanding of individual ethical principles such as transparency from different perspectives and explore regional, social and political differences. Furthermore, there is the continuous question of what role ethical concerns play in decisions of direct investment and public funding of AI research and how can they more effectively promote a responsible AI agenda.

Nevertheless, the different contributions in the book offer a multi-disciplinary and global perspective on the topic of AI ethics and touch upon three shared salient themes. First, AI ethics are not static in terms of both place and time. That means for establishing a global set of ethical AI principles it is not only necessary but rewarding to include the diversity of perspectives from all over the world. As of now, there is an imbalance that favors the perspective of the Global North. However, AI ethics are unlikely to become commonly accepted if the policy-makers, businesses and practitioners who develop, use and procure AI solutions are not involved. Moreover, AI ethics keep changing and evolving. Inclusive approaches such as the consultation processes of the UNESCO AI Recommendation or the Smart Africa AI Blueprint are laudable. But they will not be definitive because of changing technological possibilities and norms. A regular multi-stakeholder format would be able to address this and debate and adapt AI ethics based on practical experience. The Global Partnership on AI (GPAI) is one format that has the potential to grow into such an inclusive forum if it chooses to do so. Second, institutions of higher education play an important role in shaping AI practitioners who are aware of the risks and ethical dimensions of AI development. This is true for relevant programs such as Computer Science but also related fields given that AI is a cross-sectional technology. Already today AI ethics permeate all sectors and levels in that it becomes a topic for international government negotiations, business organizations and individual AI developers. Third, the teaching of AI ethics needs practical application elements. As the authors have shown ethics are a complex field of study that is intertwined with diverse traditions of thought and local context. They offer concrete recommendations on how to make AI ethics matter. In addition to institutional changes, they propose to use real-world examples and case studies in the classroom to illustrate ethical dilemmas and discuss and discover new ways to mitigate risks. Taken together, the authors add to diversifying the global debate on AI ethics and offer valuable advice to fellow lecturers, students and policy-makers alike.

References

Acuto, M., and S. Curtis. 2014. Assemblage Thinking in International Relations. In *Reassembling International Theory: Assemblage Thinking and International Relations*, ed. M. Acuto and S. Curtis, 1–16. New York: Palgrave Macmillan.

Bhardwaj, B. 2018. How AI Is Transforming The Future Of Healthcare. *Forbes*. https://www.forbes.com/sites/forbestechcouncil/2018/01/30/how-ai-is-transforming-the-future-of-healthcare/.

Chandran, R. 2022. Surveillance Hotspot, Hyderabad, Sees Facial Recognition Taken to Court. *The Economic Times*. https://economictimes.indiatimes.com/news/india/surveillance-hotspot-hyderabad-sees-facial-recognition-taken-to-court/articleshow/89007252.cms.

Chaturvedi, A., Ramdas, V., Mishra, P., and Jain, N. 2021. *Handbook on Data Protection and Privacy for Developers of Artificial Intelligence (AI) in India: Practical Guidelines for Responsible Development of AI*. GIZ: New Delhi. https://toolkit-digitalisierung.de/app/uploads/2021/07/GIZ-AI-Handbook-Report-July-2021-Final-1.pdf.

Cornet, A., Kässer, M., Müller, T., and Tschiesner, A. 2017. The Road to Artificial Intelligence Mobility—Smart Moves Required. *McKinsey Center for Future Mobility*. https://www.mckinsey.de/~/media/McKinsey/Industries/Automotive%20and%20Assembly/Our%20Insights/The%20road%20to%20artificial%20intelligence%20in%20mobility%20smart%20moves%20required/The-road-to-artificial-intelligence-in-mobility-smart-moves-required.pdf.

Digital Principles. n.d. Principles for Digital Development. https://digitalprinciples.org/.

G20. 2019. G20 AI Principles. https://www.g20-insights.org/wp-content/uploads/2019/07/G20-Japan-AI-Principles.pdf.

Guynn, J. 2019. The Problem with AI? Study Says it's Too white and Male, Calls for More Women, Minorities. *USA Today*. https://eu.usatoday.com/story/tech/2019/04/17/ai-too-white-male-more-women-minorities-needed-facial-recognition/3451932002/.

Latour, B. 2005. *Reassembling the Social: An Introduction to Actor-Network-Theory*. Oxford: Oxford University Press.

Leslie, D. 2019. Understanding artificial intelligence ethics and safety: A guide for the responsible design and implementation of AI systems in the public sector. *The Alan Turing Institute*. https://doi.org/10.5281/zenodo.3240529.

Lohr, S. 2018. Facial Recognition Is Accurate, if You're a White Guy. *New York Times*. https://www.nytimes.com/2018/02/09/technology/facial-recognition-race-artificial-intelligence.html.

OECD [Organization for Economic Cooperation and Development]. 2019. Recommendation of the Council on Artificial Intelligence. OECD/LEGAL/0449. https://legalinstruments.oecd.org/en/instruments/OECD-LEGAL-0449.

OECD [Organization for Economic Cooperation and Development]. 2022. OECD Framework for the Classification of AI Systems. *OECD Digital Economy Papers*, No. 323. https://doi.org/10.1787/cb6d9eca-en.

Smart Africa. 2021. AI for Africa Blueprint. https://smart.africa/board/login/uploads/70029-eng_ai-for-africa-blueprint.pdf.

UNESCO [United Nations Educational, Scientific and Cultural Organization]. 2021. Recommendation on the ethics of artificial intelligence. SHS/BIO/REC-AIETHICS/2021. https://unesdoc.unesco.org/ark:/48223/pf0000380455.

Vinuesa, R., Azizpour, H, Leite, I., Balaam, M., Dignum, V., Domisch, S., Felländer, A., Langhans, S.D., Tegmark, M., and Fuso Nerini, F. 2020. The role of artificial intelligence in achieving the Sustainable Development Goals. *Nature Communications* 11(233). https://doi.org/10.1038/s41467-019-14108-y.

Open Access This chapter is licensed under the terms of the Creative Commons Attribution 4.0 International License (http://creativecommons.org/licenses/by/4.0/), which permits use, sharing, adaptation, distribution and reproduction in any medium or format, as long as you give appropriate credit to the original author(s) and the source, provide a link to the Creative Commons license and indicate if changes were made.

The images or other third party material in this chapter are included in the chapter's Creative Commons license, unless indicated otherwise in a credit line to the material. If material is not included in the chapter's Creative Commons license and your intended use is not permitted by statutory regulation or exceeds the permitted use, you will need to obtain permission directly from the copyright holder.

Theoretical Underpinnings of AI Ethics in Practice

Teaching Ethics Applied to AI from a Cultural Standpoint: What African "AI Ethics" for Africa?

Emmanuel R. Goffi

Ethics applied to Artificial Intelligence (AI), improperly called AI ethics, is mainly addressed through a Western perspective focusing on continental philosophy. As a result, discussions on ethics applied to AI are shaped by the West. Consequently, the majority of AI ethical regulations are set in the West, by the West (Jobin et al. 2019). In the realm of ethics applied to AI some areas of the world are almost totally absent from the debate, Africa being the most illustrative case. Yet, diversity which makes the richness of our world should be translated into a cross-cultural approach of ethics applied to AI. As Séverine Kodjo-Grandvaux (2011) wrote it, "thinking African philosophy could lead the Western thinker to question his own philosophy and to take a self-reflexive look at his legacy".

Much greater diversity in how we approach ethics applied to AI is urgently required to represent the world's plurality of perspectives. In that sense, a culture-grounded study of ethics and its applications to AI should irrigate any teaching pertaining to the subject.

Short of a wider analysis on ethics applied to AI, we are taking the risk to fall into the trap of some kind of ethical tyranny coming from the West (Goffi 2021b) and ignoring the variety of thoughts that could be used in a global debate.

As Alassane Ndaw (2011) rightly asserted it, "being a philosopher in Africa is about understanding that there cannot be a monopoly on philosophy". Teaching diversity is a way to break this monopoly and give African philosophies and wisdoms the place they deserve in the ethical assessment of AI.

There is an African saying stating that "the sage is the one who perceives a river from the top of the trees". From the top of Western philosophical convictions, it be worth having a closer look at the river of African ethical thoughts.

E. R. Goffi (✉)
CEST – Centro de Estudos Sociedade e Tecnologia, Global AI Ethics Institute, Universidade de São Paulo, São Paulo, Brazil

Equipe Éthique, Langue, Communication et Numérique (ELCN), Université Mohammed Premier, Oujda, Morocco

© The Author(s) 2023
C. C. Corrigan et al. (eds.), *AI Ethics in Higher Education: Insights from Africa and Beyond*, SpringerBriefs in Ethics, https://doi.org/10.1007/978-3-031-23035-6_2

Representing 16% of humanity with a huge demographic potential, Africa cannot be ignored. The continent must have a say in the debate on ethics applied to AI. But, in order to enter the debate, the need for education in this specific and promising field is more than ever striking. Africa should not be given a seat at the table: it should bring its own seat and table. In other words, the continent needs to develop its own perspectives and then participate to the global debate. Thus, it will establish standards relevant to its specificities, and inform the rest of the world about divergent perspectives on ethics applied to AI. Doing so it could shape the debate on a global governance of AI and its ethical dimension, instead of enduring the Western universalist perspective.

The debate on ethics applied to AI can only be enriched with new perspectives stemming from the richness and diversity of the African continent. This open mindedness is all the more important as it would open new fields of reflections fed by mindsets and cultures. It would also undoubtedly open new perspectives that could help in establishing a fair AI governance that would be grounded in the respect of cultural diversity instead of being imposed by the West based on the disputable assumption of the existence of universal values.

This chapter, aims at opening a debate on the significance of cultures in the ethical assessment of AI, stressing the role Africa could play in the field. We will first go through a general overview of the existing normative tools, showing that they are mostly produced by Western countries. We will then have a critical look at the African awakening in the field of AI. We will finish by stressing the pressing need for much more African perspectives and initiatives in the field of ethics applied to AI, and by asserting the fundamental importance of education to train future African leaders in ethics applied to AI.

1 The Global North Versus the Global South: History Repeating?

It has become a truism to assert that AI is everywhere, even if it is not exactly true. It is becoming a truism to say that ethics is everywhere as well when it comes to AI. Short of legal tools, ethics appeared as a normative consolation solution to frame and regulate the development and use of AI systems (AIS). Yet, regulation through ethics is not enough. First, it is not supported by sanctions decided by a normative body or an official regulatory system. Second, ethics is a poorly defined notion that can be subject to many interpretations. Third, a direct consequence of the previous, is that it is too flexible a notion to be applied evenly and efficiently.

Nonetheless, this flexibility and ill-defined character are assets for stakeholders that do not want to be formally constrained by legal rules (Fjeld et al. 2015; Greene et al. 2019). In other words, ethics is the easy way to set standards without setting coercing rules, to regulate AI avoiding legally binding instruments.

Then, doors are open for norm entrepreneurs to start a "moral crusade" (Becker 1963) using norms as a tool to gain power and to protect specific interests. This race for normative power, well-illustrated by the European Union's efforts to impose rules applied to AI to the rest of the world, has led to the multiplication of codes of ethics and other ethical regulations applied to AI (Goffi et al. 2021; Goffi and Momcilovic 2021).

Yet, those crusaders are drowning the field of AI under hundreds of codes of ethics supposed to regulate its development and use. Doing so they are multiplying sources of norms making them unreadable and then ineffective. Thus, the number of ethical guidelines related to AI has grown in a concerning way these past four years or so.

A quick look at the state of the art suffices to notice the pre-eminence of the West in providing ethical norms. The number of codes pertaining to ethical standards in the field of AI has literally exploded in the past five years or so. Depending on the sources and methods, figures go from around a hundred (Dynamics of Principles Toolbox of the AI Ethics Lab; Council of Europe Digital Policies Framework) to more than a thousand normative documents (Jobin et al. 2019). The vast majority of which were established by Western countries (North America and Europe), by private companies and political bodies (Fjeld et al. 2015; Jobin et al. 2019).

Consequently, one can easily infer that there is a strong probability that existing codes of ethics applied to AI are set in a way that they support Western vested interests (Zeng et al. 2018; Hagendorf 2020). It can also be deduced that the norms established as a result are based on Western concerns presented as universal. The need for privacy would be an interesting if not enlightening case study showing that this need is not universally shared, and that privacy is not understood the same way worldwide. For example, "Ubuntu emphasizes transparency to group members, rather than individual privacy" (Dorine van Norren 2020). Consequently, there might be some legitimate doubts regarding the universal relevance and impact of these codes.

To counter these doubts, the only way is to embrace diversity, to accept that even if we ontologically share a universal belonging to the world, we might differ in our ethical views and appraisals. Then, each culture should be entitled to have its own code of ethics applied to AI, built on its own concerns, and protecting its own interests.

Yet, many parts of the world are excluded, explicitly or implicitly, from the debate on ethics applied to AI. For instance, China, which represents 20% of the world population and is aiming at being the leader in AI by 2040, is barely present in the debate on ethics applied to AI. India, with its 1.36 billion inhabitants is almost totally absent. Latin America is struggling to carve out a niche for itself in the field. The Middle East is slowly emerging trying to be heard in the Western ethical noise. Not to mention Russia.

What about Africa then? As the study by Jobin et al. mentioned it, Africa is "not represented independently from international or supranational organizations", which makes AI ethical regulations problematic for many reasons. First, these regulations might address Western concerns much more than African ones. Second, they might mostly protect Western interests and barely African ones. Third, without Africa being fully engaged in the debate, skills and knowledge will remain on the Western side and Africa's influence will remain limited. One can argue that since Africa is present in international fora, it demonstrates it is involved in the AI ethical regulation debate.

However, the play of diplomatic talks, the competitive geopolitical environment, and the interests at stake (Thibout 2019; Goffi 2020b), along with conformism that is at play among diplomats, do not allow to assert that African peoples' voices are either heard, or even correctly represented.

At the end of the day, while widely praised, diversity and its implications in the field of ethics seem to be denied in the field of AI. Ethical reflections are thus conducted like if the West had a monopoly over what is acceptable and what is not. Interestingly even the fact that some viewpoints are not mainstream is deemed unacceptable from this stance. In other words, we in the West act as if we were legitimate to judge upon the level of acceptability of ethical stances.

The question remains open: can diversity regarding ethical perspectives be denied in the name of a quest for universal standards? Making a choice between relativism and the acknowledgment that all ethical standpoints are equal and universalism and its tyrannical, not to say colonial, potential is cornelian. A third option might be interesting: the recognition of the importance of the respect we owe to particularisms stemming from cultural diversity. Thus, we could find a middle way between the excesses of both relativism and universalism, and thus avoid a new "Western cultural hegemony" (Elmandjra 1995) conveyed in a technological Trojan horse.

Africa could be the herald of such a balanced approach based on mutual listening and respect for cultural features.

2 The "Awakening" of Africa

Looking closer we can perceive some slight changes. Indeed, some countries in Africa have perfectly understood the importance of both AI and the need to be part of the AI race.

AI related technologies are slowly spreading throughout the continent. In the financial sector, for instance, young African companies are using mobile phone platforms relying on AI to provide consumers with bank services. Also, in agriculture where mobile phones are used to monitor crops growing and livestock farming, or like in Uganda, to model crops diseases. Furthermore, Africa "has seen the highest rate of increase in internet use and connectivity in the world over the last two decades" (Hafez 2020), and the potential for further improvement is indisputable with projects such as the Digital Moonshot Initiative aiming at digitally enabling the whole continent by 2030, or the African Union's Digital Transformation Agenda aspiring to allow businesses and individuals to access the Internet for free by 2030.

Nonetheless, it is essential to remember that the spreading of technology is quite uneven in Africa (Hu et al. 2019; UNESCO 2021), with for instance, an internet penetration ranging "from 55% in southern Africa to 12% in the central region of the continent" or mobile subscriptions representing "149% of the population in southern Africa and 102% in northern Africa but only 50% in central Africa" (Dannouni et al. 2020). There is a lot of work ahead to fix this digital divide, but AI remains a top priority for many countries in Africa (Asmal et al. 2020), the dynamics is there and so are the resources, even if still insufficient.

This uneven pervasiveness of AI must also be put in a wider context of profound cultural diversity on the continent (Gwagwa et al. 2020). It is thus important to stress that Africa is not one homogenous mass. It is multiple. It is a huge mosaic of ethnic cultures made of 48 mainland and 6 islands countries and some 3,000 tribes, speaking between 1,500 and 2,000 languages, and representing about 16% of the world population. The African continent is no more uniform than Europe, the Western world, the Middle East, or Latin America. Then one must bear in mind that talking about Africa as a single entity can be misleading.

This diversity is both a drawback and an asset in Africa's journey towards AI ethical regulations. A drawback first since it means that compromises must be found to allow Africa to speak in unison, if all stakeholders are ever willing to. Obviously, such a goal does not go without difficulties. The very relevance of having one voice for the whole continent is as much disputable as the universalist design of the West. However, if the European Union, despite its internal divergences, is able to reach a middle ground on the subject, one might be optimistic that Africa could succeed as well (Gwagwa et al. 2021; UNESCO 2021).

In Africa, countries such as Kenya, Tunisia, South Africa, Ghana, or Uganda are already working to develop data protection and ethics strategies. The critical question now is: Which ethical approaches are relevant in the context of the diversity the African continent is made of? It is obvious that South African expectations regarding AI (Schoeman et al. 2017) and potential regulations (UNESCO 2021) may not be the same as Nigeria's ones, that Morocco's ambitions may differ from those of Kenya, not to mention their disparate respective capacities to develop standards. When it comes to AI ethical regulations, it is then fundamental to go beyond the bad habit to consider Africa as a whole, and to take into consideration its diversity and particularisms. Navigating between different wisdoms such as Ubuntu or animism, several religions and syncretism, various traditions, diverse identities stemming from numerous historical backgrounds, Africa is a patchwork of cultures that do not fit into arbitrary categories or even established borders. Adding geopolitical and political considerations, would definitely make a unified ethics difficult to delineate.

However, despite all foreseeable difficulties, the continent should consider setting its own AI ethical regulations and monitoring bodies specifically focusing on its diversity which also makes its richness. The future of AI in Africa should be African, benefiting a population which is expected to double in the next three decades.

Yet, AI ethical standards and discussion are still set in the West as if Africa was unable to identify its own specific needs, define its own solutions, and build its own ethical framework. Africa has a lot to bring to the debate on ethics applied to AI opening doors to new perspectives stemming from its own experiences and philosophical traditions. Enriched by its exceptional spiritual diversity made of traditional Religions of the Book, wisdom such as Ubuntu and animism and its syncretic practices, African peoples have the power to help us to take a fresh look at ethics applied to

AI. An African perspective on ethics applied to AI would not only shake our conviction and open a new path towards AI ethical regulations, but it would also offer the continent normative tools fitting its very needs for the benefit of its population.

AI is not developing at the same pace in Africa as in the global North. It is undeniable that initiatives, such as the Responsible AI Network—frica, have been launched to bring Africa back in the AI race. Still, there is some work ahead if the African continent wants to take a role in AI at large, and in ethics applied to AI specifically.

One of the biggest challenges will be then to develop a native perspective on ethics applied to AI. This will not be an easy task. However, it is an essential one. Cultures, histories, religions, political systems, identities, geopolitical considerations, technological advancement, and financial interests are among some of the hurdles that Africa will have to go over to set its own ethical regulations. Africa will actually have to deal with the same difficulties to build common ethical norms than ones the rest of the world is currently experiencing, internal competitions and vested interests coming first.

As Gwagwa (2019) stresses, "despite the clear need to understand how AI affects people around the world, a truly global perspective remains a critical blind spot in the ethics conversation." Though, freeing from the universalist Western approach on ethics applied to AI seems difficult. Calling for inclusion of Africa in the debate instead of calling Africa to establish its own strategy on local grounds, is illustrative of this tendency to leave the lead to the West and to request others to join the bandwagon. Thus, while underlining the global ethical perspective blind spot, Gwagwa writes that "[e]thical AI requires the application of universal human values and international standards", adding that "[h]owever, it also needs to take into account Africa's historical peculiarities."

Africa needs more than ever to free itself from the Western universalist tropism to focus on its peoples' needs and ethical stances. Calling at the same time for universal normative standards, and for the respect of particularisms will inevitably lead to dead ends and slow down Africa's journey towards AI and its potential benefits.

The perceptible awakening of Africa in the field of AI needs to be nuanced. If there are some positive signs showing that the continent is aware of the importance and of the potential of AI, Africa is still lagging and Western viewpoints are still pervading, especially when it comes to establishing ethical norms. Africa needs to move from a passenger side to a driver side strategy if the continent wants to become a leader in the field.

"The race for digital advantage in Africa" (Dannouni et al. 2020) can only be won by trained people. Not only should people be trained to run the race, but they also need to be trained running on a specific ground for a specific type of race. In other words, when it comes to AI education, Africa should teach people to run the normative race based on cultural grounds.

3 The Importance of Africa's Native Perspective

A native perspective on ethics applied to AI is thus necessary to unleash the full potential of the continent.

In 2021 the UNESCO released the results of its *Artificial intelligence needs assessment survey in Africa*, stressing the "significant human resource gap in addressing the ethical implications of AI in the surveyed countries" and highlighting concerns regarding the safeguard of cultural heritage and the implication of AI for cultural diversity. Interestingly, the impact on cultural diversity of norms almost exclusively set by Western countries (Jobin et al. 2019) is barely addressed by scholars and commentators.

Culture here is key. Culture is the product of "the collective programming of the mind", lying on specific values and leading to appropriate behaviors (Hofstede 2001). As such cultures are the vehicle for common ideas and shared perceptions. They model communities and provide them with the necessary cement to build a society. They also provide members of the community with a sense of belonging, a structure within which individuals will build their identities and roles, which will in turn give birth to particular "expectations and meanings" that will "form a set of standards that guide behavior" (Burke and Stets 2000). As such, culture is an essential component of societies worth being protected. When it comes to AI ethical standards, if we agree that these standards are the product of culture, we might assume that they will differ from one cultural community to another. This diversity and the range of particularisms it covers need to be defended against any attempt to impose standards, legal and/or ethical, from the outgroups. Cultural diversity and particularisms must be fully considered and integrated into the debate on ethics applied to AI (Goffi 2021a, b). More than just an option, it must be seen as a "matter of survival" (Elmandjra 1995).

Incidentally, the fundamental value of cultural diversity is clearly and loudly stated in the Universal Declaration of Human Rights (art. 22) and the Universal Declaration on Cultural Diversity (art. 4), of the United Nations Educational, Scientific and Cultural Organization adopted in 2001. The United Nations Charter, furthermore, calls for international co-operation in the cultural field (art. 13) and for "international cultural and educational cooperation" (art. 55), "with due respect for the culture" of the peoples (art. 73).

Aside from "culture", keywords here are "cooperation" and "respect". Respectful cooperation in the field of ethics applied to AI cannot go through mere inclusion of the African continent into an existing debate of which limits have been mainly set by Western countries. A call for inclusion presupposes exclusion and can even lead to more exclusion. By setting standards without listening to African voices, "the Global North may lead the social inclusion discourse and take decisions on how African civil society should be included" (Gwagwa 2019). Such a situation would eventually lead to the denial of Africa's right to make its own way towards its own AI ethical regulations, excluding de facto the continent from the debate. On the other hand, it must be recognized that African actors need to develop their own perspective as independently as possible from Western influences. Thus, instead of assessing "the extent to which Africa has been included in the AI ethics discussions to date" (Gwagwa 2019), it is worth assessing what Africa's peoples are and what native solutions might be offered.

Africa should from now on consider developing standards fitting its needs and its cultures. This will be possible if and only if education on native ethical perspectives is developed at all levels from initial to continuing education.

So far, Africa has been following, sometimes from afar, the discussion on ethics applied to AI. Most of the initiatives that are launched in the field of AI in Africa are actually initiated by Western institutions or under the auspices of international organizations such as the UNESCO, where the play of diplomacy and the level of conformism does not allow the expression of grass roots' viewpoints.

African trailblazers in ethics applied to AI will then emerge from the youngest generation that will be educated on the subject from their respective cultural standpoints. This is exactly the claim made by the UNESCO's Director-General when she asserts that "we must empower young people by providing them with the skills they need for life in the twenty-first century" and eventually "to ensure that Africa fully participates in transformations related to AI, not only as a beneficiary but also upstream, contributing directly to its development" (Azoulay n.d.).

Yet, behind good intentions bad methods can be found, and even if the UNESCO aims at being "a universal forum where everyone's voice is heard and respected" (Azoulay n.d.) it does not mean that everyone's voice is actually heard and respected.

Indeed, Azoulay (n.d.), while calling for an international dialogue, also states that ethics applied to AI is a global issue and that "reflection on it must take place at the global level so as to avoid a 'pick-and-choose' approach to ethics". The problem with such a statement is that it closes doors to particularisms trying to merge diverse and intricate perspectives into one single stance. The very ethical question here would be to know why "a 'pick-and-choose' approach to ethics", which refers to the idea that each actor should be entitled to take whatever it considers as relevant to its specific case, should be avoided. Then the very fact that ethics applied to AI is a global issue is misleading for in many places around the world, it is not even a subject either because it is not culturally necessary (for instance in culture where ethics is based on religious beliefs that cannot be questioned by regular people), or because technology is not seen as problematic, or even because technology is not accessible.

So, questions remain open: on what ethical ground can we assert that 'pick-and-choose' ethics are less acceptable than global ethics? Isn't respect for diversity, including ethical diversity, a value for the UNESCO? Is relativism more unacceptable ethically than universal hegemony?

As philosopher Effa (2015), writing on animism, puts it, "Africa has still a lot to tell us. Since she went through the great ordeal, she is in some ways enlightened (*initiée*)". The very first thing Africa could offer to the world is a unique perspective, maybe more pragmatic, on ethics applied to AI. Developing its own ethical perspective, Africa could participate to the setting of a global governance system that would take into account the specificities of the continent.

As an illustration, Gwagwa (2019) relevantly stresses, that "governments of the Global North, with some exceptions, mostly approach the ownership and protection of data simply from a personal privacy angle, without considering the economic value of processed and redacted data, whilst those in the Global South are only beginning to see such datasets as a valuable collective informational resource". Africa might initiate a debate on what privacy really means for African people since "[a]n African approach to privacy and protection is not about personal data, but collective rights" (Romanoff and Hidalgo-Sanchis 2019). Then it should evaluate the importance of privacy compared to the expected economic gains related to the use of data potentially seeing them as a "promising resource" (Goffi 2020a) in the struggle between multinational companies and African actors (Dannouni et al. 2020). The ethical perspective might be then quite different and so would be standards.

As a consequence, "[f]uture regulatory frameworks should not merely be imported from the West as policy transfer but engaged with and adapted to the African context" (Gwagwa 2019) and interests.

What is needed now in Africa, is a huge education program providing peoples with the relevant tools to make their own opinion on what they need and how they want to reach their goals within a specific cultural ethical framework. Equipped with such skills, African peoples will be able to not be included into an existing debate, but to initiate new debates and thus have a real influence at the global level on the future of AI and its normative frame.

Eventually, education at large, and critical thinking specifically, is the key that will open the door to autonomous reflections on ethics applied to AI in Africa and allow the continent to develop and use AI *for* Africans in an ethically acceptable and unbiased way.

4 Education: A Necessary Tool for Africa's Influence in Ethics Applied to AI

Following Swiss psychologist Jean (1990, 1952, 1997), Piaget and Inhelder (1969) works on cognitive development, and Russian psychologist Vygotsky (1978, 1986) writings on the impact of social interactions on cognition and behaviour, social constructivists have demonstrated the importance of culture in the shaping of ideas. If Piaget's and Vygotsky's research focused on children, they can nonetheless be extended to adults whose perceptions of the world are influenced by their experiences and consequently by their early education.

Then social constructivism has been extensively used in the field of education explaining how learners are constructing their knowledge based on experiences. Stating that reality is a social construction (Berger and Luckmann 1966), constructivists offer a method to understand how this reality is built.

Two elements seem essential to stress regarding ethics applied to AI from an African perspective. First, according to social constructivism, education is the vehicle for the construction of both morality and the reality of the world. Second, language plays a critical role in spreading ideas and thus shaping perceptions.

If we agree with Durkheim (1925) that education, including moral education, and language are both intrinsically linked to culture, this leads us to postulate that any fair ethical appraisal of AI should stem from a specific education and language, in other words from a specific cultural standpoint.

Consequently, education based on local cultural standards is essential to the protection of culture. Conversely, any education based on outgroups cultural standards could lead to some kind of weakening if not disappearance of a specific culture. As Durkheim asserted it "[w]henever two peoples, two groups of individuals belonging to different levels of culture, are brought into continuous contact with each other, certain feelings will develop which will make the group which has or believes itself to have the higher culture tend to do violence to the other group" (Durkheim 1925). Even if Durkheim deducted this law from the specific case of corporal punishment in school settings, it is still relevant considering that the denial of cultural particularism can be likened to a form of psychological violence, sometimes, as History as unfortunately shown, leading to physical violence.

Yet, as stated in the UNESCO's Universal Declaration on Cultural Diversity, "[t]he defence of cultural diversity is an ethical imperative, inseparable from respect for human dignity" (art. 4), and "due respect for the culture" of the peoples is a legal requirement enshrined in the United Nations Charter.

Therefore, adopting ethical rules applicable to AI set by Western countries seems not only irrelevant regarding respect for cultural diversity, but it also seems potentially dangerous for African people. Yet, the tendency is still to ask for help in terms of setting standards (UNESCO 2021).

5 Facing the Turning Point: Towards Conformism or Towards Autonomy

Two alternatives lie before Africa today. On the one hand, the continent can keep on calling for inclusion into the existing debate framed by Western actors and adopting pre-established normative instruments and reflections trying to adjust them to its needs. Doing so, Africa would recognize the influence of other cultures on its own ones, and thus accept the potential risks for its cultures. Falling into "moral realism" (Piaget 1997), i.e. the idea that rules define what is right and what is wrong and that "[a]ny act that shows obedience to a rule (...) is good; any act that does not conform to rules is bad", would lead to the mere application of Western standards to African situations, with the risk that these standards would not benefit Africa's peoples.

On the other hand, Africa could start working on a native "construction of reality" grounded on its own experiences and needs. It would then free itself from the Western moral tutelage. This second option is by far the most relevant if African countries want to fully benefit from the godsend of AI and be competitive at the international level.

Then the very first step would be to educate people in Africa in a way that would empower them with the sufficient knowledge and skills to take charge of their own fortune. Such an education should be built upon a constructivist approach considering, first, that knowledge is the product of experiences rooted in specific contexts and of social processes and interactions, second, that it results from language use, itself integrated in a cultural setting.

Teaching should not be reduced to mere spreading of existing knowledge. It should challenge learners, give them a voice, support them in making their own theories, building their own perceptions. It should also be contextualized in order to offer students with a full understanding of the context in which ethics applied to AI is implemented. Passive learning, consisting in waiting for the West to provide knowledge, must yield priority to active learning empowering learners with necessary skills to construct native meanings through active engagement with their cultural environment. Putting down learners' roots in a community sharing values and ideas will provide them with a sense of belonging, with a role and identity (Burke and Stets 2000), and help them to acquire meaning "in a system of social behavior" (Vygotsky 1978).

The above-mentioned need for educational shift perfectly aligns with the survey released by the UNESCO (2021), stressing that 84 percent of responding African countries consider that "updating education, skills and training systems to strengthen human and institutional capacities for the development and use of AI" is important.

Educational strategies must be developed in Africa to avoid "moral crusaders" (Becker 1963) to impact local cultures. Once again, the UNESCO's (2021) survey stresses that "[t]he implications of AI for cultural diversity is important for 20 countries, of which ten consider the issue to be urgent" but does not mention potential risks associated with the imposition of non-African moral standards to the continent and the need for native reflections on ethics applied to AI.

Africa has a unique opportunity to make its own journey towards AI and its ethical framework. What it needs is to develop a "theory of experience" rooted in its own settings to move "forward to ever greater utilization of scientific method in the development of the possibilities of growing, expanding experience" (Dewey 1938).

As Honebein (1996) summarized it, such a strategy should aim at reaching several pedagogical goals, among which embedding "learning in realistic and relevant contexts" and grounding it "problems within the noise and complexity that surrounds them".

Education in Africa should be aimed at solving African problems through African reflections based on African cultural perspectives and identified needs. Any attempts to adjust Western standards to the African situation is a risky bet. Ethics applied to AI is no exception. It is all the more relevant that ethics is based on values that are themselves grounded into culture.

6 Conclusion

The wideness of the world barely falls in with the narrowness of our mindsets. Education is a way to open our mind to diversity and to listen to particular perspectives.

Clearly, AI has an enormous potential to generate wealth in Africa. However, framing this potential within ethical standards set by non-African stakeholders may hinder the expected benefits of AI for the continent. Undoubtedly, Africa as a tessellated area will face internal struggles around vested interests related to AI foreseeable godsends. Yet, it might be easier and more relevant to find a compromise, even if unperfect, on AI ethical norms between African actors than to import existing frameworks that would not fit Africa's needs and would potentially jeopardize its expected benefits. So far, the West is leading the normative debate on AI shaping its outlines and slowly imposing its perspective without due consideration of the cultural diversity of ethical stances.

Africa needs to shift to many native educational strategies aiming at empowering its people and providing them with all necessary skills and tools to be competitive in the international AI race.

Things are evolving at a slow pace in Africa. Even if the continent is perfectly aware of the benefits it could withdraw from AI, it is still lagging waiting for inclusion into the ethical debate. Short of a native perspective, African countries are relying on existing codes and normative documents established by non-African countries. Adopting standards set in a different cultural environment might be dangerous for it would give room to cultural influence that might endanger African cultures.

References

Asmal, Zaakhir, Begashaw, Belay, and Bhorat, Haroon et al. 2020. Foresight Africa: Top Priorities for the Continent 2020–2030. *Africa Growth Initiative at Brookings*. https://www.brookings.edu/wp-content/uploads/2020/01/ForesightAfrica2020_20200110.pdf.

Azoulay, Audrey. n.d. Towards an Ethics of Artificial Intelligence. *United Nations—UN Chronicle*. https://www.un.org/en/chronicle/article/towards-ethics-artificial-intelligence.

Becker, Howard S. 1963. *Outsiders: Studies in the Sociology of Deviance*. The Free Press.

Berger, Peter L., and Luckmann, Thomas. 1966. *The Social Construction of Reality: A Treatise in the Sociology of Knowledge*. Penguin Books.

Burke, Peter J., and Jan E. Stets. 2000. Identity Theory and Social Identity Theory. *Social Psychology Quarterly* 63 (3): 224–237.

Dannouni, Amane, Maher, Hamid, and Gildemeister Jan, et al. 2020. The Race for Digital Advantage in Africa. *Boston Cosulting Group*. https://www.bcg.com/publications/2020/race-digital-advantage-in-africa.

Dewey, John. 1938. *Experience and Education*. Free Press.

Dorine van Norren. 2020. *The ethics of AI and Ubuntu*. Paper presentation at "Africa Knows" Conference.

Durkheim, Emile. 1925. *L'éducation morale*. Félix Alcan.

Effa, Gaston-Paul. 2015. *Le dieu perdu dans l'herbe: L'animisme, une philosophe africaine*. Presses du Châtelet.
Elmandjra, Mahdi. 1995. Diversité culturelle: Une question de survie. *Futuribles analyse et prospective* 202: 5–15.
Fjeld, Jessica, Achten, Nele, Hilligoss, Hannah, Nagy, Adam, Adam, and Srikumar, Madhulika. 2015. Principled Artificial Intelligence: Mapping Consensus in Ethical and Rights-Based Approaches to Principles for AI. *Berkman Klein Center Research Publication*, 2020.1.
Ghanem, Hafez. 2020. Shooting for the moon: An agenda to Bridge Africa's Digital Divide. *Brookings* Foresight Africa 2020 series. https://www.brookings.edu/blog/africa-in-focus/2020/02/07/shooting-for-the-moon-an-agenda-to-bridge-africas-digital-divide/.
Goffi, Emmanuel R. 2020a. Data: The New Strategic Resource. *Institut Sapiens*. https://www.institutsapiens.fr/data-the-new-strategic-resource/.
Goffi, Emmanuel R. 2020b. L'intelligence artificielle comme facteur de puissance internationale. *Diplomatie* 104: 82–84.
Goffi, Emmanuel R. 2021a. Escaping the Western Cosm-Ethical Hegemony: The Importance of Cultural Diversity in the Ethical Assessment of Artificial Intelligence. *AI Ethics Journal*. https://www.aiethicsjournal.org/10-47289-aiej2021a0716-1.
Goffi, Emmanuel R. 2021b. The importance of cultural diversity in AI ethics. *ISSG—Beyond The Horizon*. https://horizonglobalacademy.eu/the-importance-of-cultural-diversity-in-ai-ethics/.
Goffi, Emmanuel R., and Momcilovic, Aco. 2021. Too Many Norms Kill Norms: The EU Normative Hemorrhage. *ISSG—Beyond The Horizon*. https://behorizon.org/too-many-norms-kill-norms-the-eu-normative-hemorrhage/.
Goffi, Emmanuel R., Colin, Louis, and Belouali, Saida. 2021. Ethical Assessment of AI Cannot Ignore Cultural Pluralism: A Call for Broader Perspective on AI Ethics. *Human Rights in Africa & the Mediterranean International Journal* 48–71.
Greene, Daniel, Hoffmann, Anna Lauren, and Stark, Luke. 2019. Better, Nicer, Clearer, Fairer: A Critical Assessment of the Movement for Ethical Artificial Intelligence and Machine Learning. *HICSS*.
Gwagwa, Arthur, Kachidza, Patti, and Siminyu, Kathleen, et al. 2021. Responsible Artificial Intelligence in Sub-Saharan Africa: Landscape and General State of Play. *Artificial Intelligence for Development Africa*. https://ircai.org/wp-content/uploads/2021/03/AI4D_Report_Responsible_AI_in_SSA.pdf.
Gwagwa, Arthur, Kraemer-MbulaII, Erika, and Rizk III, Nagla, et al. 2020. Artificial Intelligence (AI) Deployments in Africa: Benefits, Challenges and Policy Dimensions. *The African Journal of Information and Communication* 26. http://www.scielo.org.za/scielo.php?script=sci_arttext&pid=S2077-72132020000200002.
Gwagwa, Arthur. 2019. Recommendations on the inclusion sub-Saharan Africa in Global AI Ethics. RANITP Policy Brief 2, *Research ICT Africa*. https://researchictafrica.net/wp-content/uploads/2020/11/RANITP2019-2-AI-Ethics.pdf.
Hagendorf, Thilo. 2020. The Ethics of AI Ethics: An Evaluation of Guidelines. *Minds and Machines* 30: 99–120. https://link.springer.com/content/pdf/https://doi.org/10.1007/s11023-020-09517-8.pdf
Hofstede, Geert. 2001. *Culture's Consequences: Comparing Values, Behaviors, Institutions, and Organizations Across Nations*. Sage Publications.
Honebein, Peter C. 1996. Seven Goals for the Design of Constructivist Learning Environments. In *Constructivist Learning Environments: Case Studies in Instructional Design*, ed. Wilson, Brent G., 11–24. Educational Technology Publications.
Hu, Xianhong, Neupane, Bhanu, and Echaiz, Lucia Flores, et al. 2019. *Steering AI and Advanced ICTs for Knowledge Societies: A Rights, Openness, Access, and Multi-stakeholder Perspective*. UNESCO. https://unesdoc.unesco.org/ark:/48223/pf0000372132.locale=en.
Jobin, Anna, Marcello Ienca, and Effy Vayena. 2019. The global landscape of AI ethics guidelines. *Nature Machine Intelligence* 1 (9): 389–399.

Kodjo-Grandvaux, Séverine. 2011. Vous avez dit "philosophie africaine"? *Critique* LXVII (771–772): 613–623.
Ndaw, Alassane. 2011. Philosopher en Afrique, c'est comprendre que nul n'a le monopole de la philosophie. *Critique* LXVII (771–772): 624–628.
Piaget, Jean. 1990. *The Child's Conception of the World*. Littlefield Adams.
Piaget, Jean. 1952. *The Origins of Intelligence in Children*. International Universities Press.
Piaget, Jean. 1997. *The Moral Judgment of the Child*. The Free Press.
Piaget, Jean, and Inhelder, Bärbel. 1969. *The Psychology of the Child*. Basic Books.
Romanoff, Mila, and Hidalgo-Sanchis, Paula. 2019. Building Ethical AI Approaches in the African Context. *UN Global Pulse*. https://www.unglobalpulse.org/2019/08/ethical-ai-approaches-in-the-african-context/.
Schoeman, Willie, Moore, Rory, and Seedat, Yusof, et al. 2017. Artificial Intelligence: Is South Africa ready? *Accenture and the University of Pretoria's Gordon Institute of Business Science*. https://www.accenture.com/_acnmedia/pdf-107/accenture-ai-south-africa-ready.pdf.
Thibout, Charles. (2019). La compétition mondiale de l'intelligence artificielle. *Pouvoirs - Revue française d'études constitutionnelles et politiques* 170 (3): 131–142.
UNESCO. 2021. *Artificial Intelligence Needs Assessment Survey in Africa*. United Nations Educational, Scientific and Cultural Organization. https://en.unesco.org/news/unesco-launches-findings-artificial-intelligence-needs-assessment-survey-africa.
Vygotsky, Lev. 1978. *Mind in Society: The Development of Higher Psychological Processes*. Harvard University Press.
Vygotsky, Lev. 1986. *Thought and Language*. MIT Press (First edited in Russian 1934).
Zeng, Yi, Lu, Enmeng, and Huangfu, Cunqing. 2018. Linking Artificial Intelligence Principles. In *CEUR Workshop Proceedings* 2301, paper 15.

Open Access This chapter is licensed under the terms of the Creative Commons Attribution 4.0 International License (http://creativecommons.org/licenses/by/4.0/), which permits use, sharing, adaptation, distribution and reproduction in any medium or format, as long as you give appropriate credit to the original author(s) and the source, provide a link to the Creative Commons license and indicate if changes were made.

The images or other third party material in this chapter are included in the chapter's Creative Commons license, unless indicated otherwise in a credit line to the material. If material is not included in the chapter's Creative Commons license and your intended use is not permitted by statutory regulation or exceeds the permitted use, you will need to obtain permission directly from the copyright holder.

Practical Implications of Different Theoretical Approaches to AI Ethics

Ugochi A. Okengwu

Ethics are moral principles that govern a person's behaviour or the conduct of an activity. As a practical example, one ethical principle is to deal with all of us with respect. Philosophers have debated that ethics for plenty centuries and there are numerous famous concepts, perhaps one of the most well-known being Kant's express imperative act as you may like every other humans to behave towards all different humans (From Kant's 1785 ebook 'Ground work of the metaphysics of morals').

Different Artificial Intelligence (AI) ethics standards, guidelines and strategies have been formulated round the world to assist remedy the rising issues of Artificial Intelligence structures in our society, like OECD (Organisation for Economic Co-operation and Development), AI4People' Ethical Frameworks, The Beijing AI Principles. Application of responsible AI in finance, area exploration, superior production, transportation, electricity improvement, Agriculture and health is a crucial aspect of growing AI systems.

We have noticed the effect of automation on "blue and white-collar" jobs, but as computer systems turn out to be very complex and useful, more jobs and positions are made obsolete. The effect of AI and robotics in Africa will lead to inequality; there will be a large quantity of unemployable humans and breakdowns in the social order (Smith and Anderson 2014). The most important question around AI is inequality, which isn't normally covered within the debate in AI ethics. It's an ethical problem, however, it's mostly an issue of politics 'who benefits from AI' (Stilgoe 2020). It has been observed that lack of government engagement to date has been a hindrance and encouraging African governments to take a proactive approach to AI policy.

In reality, possible dangers emerge from the AI race narrative, in addition to a really competitive race to develop AI systems for technological superiority (Cave and ÓhÉigeartaigh 2018). In drafting these legal guidelines, African regulators should learn from International best practices, which include warding off burdensome

---

U. A. Okengwu (✉)
Department of Computer Science, The University of Port Harcourt, Port Harcourt, Nigeria

requirements which could foreclose the benefits of AI and position African businesses at a disadvantage. Ethical techniques should remove bureaucracy that will mitigate and intervene in the long standing societal biases, mainly on the grounds of protected characteristics such as race and culture. Developing African-Centric AI models, the use of information sourced from Africa will make it easy for practical implementation of theoretical AI ethics in Africa, although UNESCO survey results shows that African countries like Congo, Sao Tome and Principe, Zimbabwe have developed ethical guidelines for AI but a general and harmonized approach is necessary to protect individuals and collective privacy rights in the cross border of AI data.

1 Ethics in Artificial Intelligence

There ought to be ideas that govern the discovery and design of Artificial intelligence agents. AI is defined as developing machines that could assume, learn and react like human (Siau and Wang 2020). We will similarly broaden the definition to describe machines that do things that could normally require human intelligence—things consisting of speech recognition, visible perception, and choice making (Siau and Wang 2020). The conduct of the scientists inventing these machines and the machines themselves can also have moral issues. In a recent managed study, researchers reviewed those moral recommendations function as a foundation for ethical decision-making for software program engineers (McNamara et al. 2018). There is poor practice of AI systems in compliance with the implementation of ethical guidelines, although there are some AI ethics frameworks formulated from different parts of the world today, namely.

1.1 OECD (Organisation for Economic Co-operation and Development)

This AI ethics framework recommended five complementary values-based principles for the responsible stewardship of trustworthy AI, which includes that AI should drive inclusive growth, sustainable development and wellbeing; AI systems development should consider rule of law, human rights, democratic values and diversity, appropriate safeguards; AI system outcomes should be transparent and properly disclosed to the users; Safety and security should be incorporated during the development plan of AI systems, finally organisations and individuals developing, deploying AI systems should be accountable to the outcome of the AI systems.

1.2 AI4People' Ethical Frameworks

This Artificial Intelligence ethics guidelines is about Human organisation and oversight which include monitoring, schooling, human-machine interfaces and external control of automobile data; Technical robustness and safety—together with resilience to assault and security, fall back plan and regular safety, accuracy and reliability; privacy and data governance together with respect for privacy, transparency & communication, and access to facts; Transparency as a key mechanism to comprehend all other requirements; Diversity, non-discrimination and equity which includes the avoidance of unfair bias, accountable balancing and accessibility; Societal and environmental wellness—including sustainability and environmental friendliness and social effect; Accountability—which includes audit ability, measures of transparency, reporting of poor effect.

1.3 The Beijing AI Principles

The creation of Artificial Intelligence (AI) worries the future of the entire society, all humankind, and the environment. The ideas are proposed right here as an initiative for the research, development, use, and governance and long-term planning of AI, calling for its healthy improvement to assist the development of a network of common destiny, and the belief of useful AI for humankind and nature. The improvement of AI have to do nicely to all mankind and conform to human values like privacy, dignity, freedom, autonomy, and rights, the developers or researchers of AI systems ought to be responsible for the outcome of their merchandise and additionally endeavour to control the activities of the AI systems to divert risk. There ought to be a reflection of diversity and inclusiveness when constructing an open AI machine. Additionally, customers of AI systems have to be taken into consideration so that they need to gain knowledge of how to use the AI systems wisely and have enough information on how the AI system affects their rights and interests. Governance of AI ought to look at Optimizing employment; concordance and cooperation need to be actively increase so one can express the philosophy of "optimizing philosophy", and long-term planning to encourage Artificial general Intelligence.

Having looked at globally present AI ethics frameworks like OECD (Organization for Economic Co-operation and Development), AI4People' ethical Frameworks, The Beijing AI principles, it's far clearly beneficial for African countries to form a unifying AI ethics framework for AI implementation to facilitate the practice of AI ethics in Africa.

2 Suggestions for Practicing AI Ethics in Africa

Practice of AI Ethics that is created with African context in Africa will definitely cause independent and complete representation of human beings from different kinds of ethnic agencies, as AI permeates our lives in Africa. Africa is a continent made up of nations with unique cultures and values. There is need to bear in mind the peculiarity of Africa when designing or developing AI Ethics for practice in Africa. The increasing adoption of AI faces certain challenges and constraints, AI and the associated strategies of machine learning, deep Learning, Data science, and so forth is based on getting access to massive quantities of facts that may help train and develop new systems. The variety and value of facts will decide what model will analyze, if the records is western way culture inclined, it will affect the outcome of the system. This imbalance carries dangers, in particular wherein the moral norms and values designed into those technologies collide with those of the African groups in which they're deployed. AI ethics which are applicable inside the context of African Continents are unique to African nations. This can be achieved through engaging in the following activities.

2.1 Defining African Values and Align AI with Such Values

Any AI project implementation should be preceded by values and risk assessment. In doing so, they should choose and contextualize only the good parts of global initiatives that accord with African own ethical values and cultural contexts. What ethics means to Africa may be different to other regions, for instance, African cultures, despite the diversity, have certain commonalities that include Ubuntu which encompasses a collective approach to life, sentimental and religious values and beliefs that include the desire for collective good outcomes while being conscious of evil, as well as a belief in life after death values, may not accord with or may even collide with African interests in the context of AI. African beliefs and values consideration, determine the type of AI that is created.

2.2 Protecting Data Privacy and Privacy Rights in Cross Border Data Flows

AI affects the privacy of individuals especially through big data: long term records that can be kept on any one who produces storable data. Digital records can be searched using algorithms for pattern recognition meaning that we have lost the default assumption of anonymity by obscurity (Selinger and Hartzog 2017). Any one of us can be identified by facial recognition software or data mining of our shopping or social media habits (Pasquale 2015). AI has been making such massive progress for several years precisely because of the large amounts of (personal) data available. Those data are collected by privacy-invasive social media platforms, Smartphone apps, as well as Internet of Things devices with their countless sensors. In the near future, vision-based drones, robots and wearable cameras may expand this surveillance to rural locations and one's home, places of worship, and places where privacy is considered sacrosanct, such as bathrooms and changing rooms. As the applications of robots and wearable cameras expand into our homes and begin to capture and record all aspects of daily living. We begin to approach a world in which all, even bystanders are being constantly observed by various cameras wherever they go (Wagner 2018). Presently, Africa is adopting AI at the stage of implementation when data is more important than the technology itself. African countries have already been working on data issues and facing data protection challenges in the process while some are in the process of coming up with a legal framework. We can conclude that the current AI boom coincides with the emergence of a post-privacy society. Collective rights of peoples and communities must be protected in addition to personal privacy. This can be achieved through the Harmonisation of Data and AI frameworks in Africa.

2.3 Ensuring Quality of Data and Removing Biases

Building AI systems, most often requires people to manage and clean up data to instruct the training algorithms with huge training data sets, the question is the sociodemographic source of this data determines how the AI model will behave. The inventor or developer of an AI has great potential to determine its use and reach (Conn 2018), suggesting a need for inventors to consider the wider impacts of their creation. AI machines use algorithms (a set of sequential rules to be followed in problem-solving) created by humans, so if the creator has any inherent biases or is judgmental in some way, those biases can be built into the machine. Imagine a machine used to predict criminal behaviour that includes the creator's bias against a particular race. That wouldn't be fair or neutral, Systematic bias may arise as a result of the data used to train systems or as a result of values held by system developers and users. Researchers have found that automated advertisement tools are more likely to distribute adverts for well-paid jobs to men than women (Datta et al. 2015). AI that is biased against particular groups within society can have far-reaching effects. Its use in law enforcement or national security, for example, could result in some demographics being unfairly imprisoned or detained. If AI is used to screen people for job applications or university admissions it could result in entire sections of society being disadvantaged. Using AI to perform credit checks could result in some individuals being unfairly refused loans, making it difficult for them to escape a cycle of poverty. However addressing the gender biases, culture biases and race biases in the development and use of AI systems will ensure AI ethics with African context, will be implemented in Africa.

2.4 Introducing Safeguards to Balance AI Opportunities and Risks

AI offers opportunities mostly in the following areas: research and innovation; smart automation in core areas such as health e.g. disease diagnostics such as malaria and TB test automation and smart involvement and participation, clerical roles, agriculture which employs 70% of Africa's labor, energy, and tourism. AI also presents opportunities for efficient public sector decisions and resource allocation especially in social protection schemes, business analytics through increased data intelligence. One way of programming AI systems is reinforcement learning where improved performance is reinforced with a virtual reward. If we consider a system to be suffering when its reward functions give it negative input, therefore once we consider machines as entities that can perceive, feel and act, it is no huge leap to ponder their legal status. In practicing AI Ethics in Africa, AI machines should not be seen as moral agency or seen as persons.

2.5 Fair and Socially Responsible AI

AI should be both fair and inclusive; taking the continent's nuances into account. This can be achieved through Use of open data sets for benchmarking fairness. The use of open data sets with safeguards offers benefits for benchmarking fairness among other purposes. Ethically built and used AI could help promote equality and fairness, but poor or malicious design risks exacerbating existing social problems in new ways. Bryson (2019) argues that giving robots moral agency could in itself be construed as an immoral action, as it would be unethical to artefacts in a situation of competition with us. Fair and socially responsible AI needs to include and embody African values.

2.6 Engaging Local Communities

The ethics of community creation goes over and above the legal requirements to include awareness-raising as a public dimension of policy: understanding the peculiar needs of the people, working that is based on dialogue with communities making sure they are included in the research, public engagement during which they can inform the experts of their unique needs, and not exploiting them or simply ticking the boxes as required by the law.

2.7 Social Inclusion of Africa in the Fourth Industrial Revolution

While AI has the potential to help solve many of humanity's most pressing problems, for example by creating a world that is less sick, less hungry, more productive, better educated, and better prepared to thwart the effects of climate change, evidence suggests that this promise comes with an escalating global risk of entrenched and amplified social inequality. The uncertainty of AI and some of its negative impact is most likely to be felt in the Global South, especially Africa who may be excluded on both social, economic, and various grounds.

3 African-Context—AI Ethics Framework

African Artificial Intelligence should follow these guidelines.

- Governments in Africa should include AI ethics practice in the government policies.
- Awareness index of AI ethics in Africa should be upgraded to a high level. To ensure AI can benefit all and create the most societal value, stakeholders need to have open conversations about the ethical dimensions of this technology and take appropriate actions.
- African values and morals should be considered when building AI systems because Africans have regard for privacy, especially sex life. So, it is against African values and morals to use sexbots which is one of the products of AI.
- Africans live communally, so local communities should be engaged while building AI systems that will be used by Africans.
- Africa AI products should not be available only to a particular set of people due to digital divide, lack of social amenities and communication facilities, this can be resolved by ensuring more investment in technology.

4 Conclusion

In Africa, AI can help with some of the region's most pervasive problems: from reducing poverty and improving education, to delivering healthcare and eradicating diseases, addressing sustainability challenges, the growing demand for food from fast-growing population to advancing inclusion in societies. AI offers vast opportunities in the area of health, transportation; education, agriculture, etc. The ethical implementation of AI faces some challenges like digital terminologies used differently in different continents, countries, and communities which could be expressed due to diversity in culture and way of life.. The digital divide, which is the gap between individuals, households, businesses and geographic areas at different socio-economic levels with regard to both their opportunities to access information and communication technologies (ICTs) and to their use of the Internet for a wide variety of activities, is also a major issue in Africa, which hinders the use of digital services like AI. As a first step in dealing with these challenges, African stakeholders should work together to ensure AI applications are developed by teams with diverse demographic, gender, ethnic, and socio-economic backgrounds. This is important to avoid cognitive bias. AI innovation will be key to solving many of these challenges as long as it integrates consideration of ethical implications of systems that they build. It's also true that the risks of AI cause human misunderstanding and overreliance on AI systems, as they also have limitations in the systems themselves. Therefore, developers must always strive to fully and effectively communicate with users and regulators to ensure adequate understanding of the technology, its use, and the risks associated with it.

References

Bryson, J.J. 2019. The Past Decade and Future of AI's Impact on Society. In *Towards a New Enlightenment? A Transcendent Decade*, eds. M. Baddeley, M. Castells, A. Guiora, N. Chau, B. Eichengreen, R. López, R., Kanbur, and V. Burkett, Madrid, Turner.

Cave, S., and S.S. ÓhÉigeartaigh. 2018. An AI Race for Strategic Advantage: Rhetoric and Risks, 1–5.

Conn, A. 2018. AI Should Provide a Shared Benefit for as Many People as Possible, Future of Life Institute. https://futureoflife.org/2018/01/10/shared-benefit-principle/. Accessed 12 Aug. 2019.

Datta, A., M.C. Tschantz, and A. Datta. 2015. Automated Experiments on Ad Privacy Settings—A Tale of Opacity, Choice, and Discrimination. In *Proceedings on Privacy Enhancing Technologies*, vol. 1, 92–112, https://doi.org/10.1515/popets-2015-0007.

McNamara, A., J. Smith, E. Murphy-Hill. 2018. Does ACM's code of ethics change ethical decision making in software development? In *Proceedings of the 2018 26th ACM joint meeting on european software engineering conference and symposium on the foundations of software engineering— ESEC/FSE*, eds. G.T. Leavens, A. Garcia, and C.S. Păsăreanu, 1–7. New York: ACM Press.

Pasquale, F. 2015. *The Black Box Society: The Secret Algorithms that Control Money and Information*. Cambridge, MA: Harvard University Press.

Selinger, Evan & Hartzog, Woodrow. (2017). Obscurity and Privacy. https://doi.org/10.4324/978 0203735657-12.

Siau, K., and W. Wang. 2020. Artificial Intelligence (AI) Ethics: Ethics of AI and Ethical AI. *Journal of Database Management (JDM)* 31 (2): 74–87. https://doi.org/10.4018/JDM.2020040105.

Smith A., J. Anderson. 2014. AI, Robotics, and the Future of Jobs, Pew Research Center. http://www.pewinternet.org/2014/08/06/future-of-jobs/.

Stilgoe, J. 2020. *Who's Driving Innovation?: New Technologies and the Collaborative State.* Palgrave Macmillan. https://doi.org/10.1007/978-3-3-030-32320-2_2.

Wagner A.R. 2018. An Autonomous Architecture that Protects the Right to Privacy. https://www.aies-conference.com/2018/contents/papers/main/AIES_2018_paper_125.pdf.

Open Access This chapter is licensed under the terms of the Creative Commons Attribution 4.0 International License (http://creativecommons.org/licenses/by/4.0/), which permits use, sharing, adaptation, distribution and reproduction in any medium or format, as long as you give appropriate credit to the original author(s) and the source, provide a link to the Creative Commons license and indicate if changes were made.

The images or other third party material in this chapter are included in the chapter's Creative Commons license, unless indicated otherwise in a credit line to the material. If material is not included in the chapter's Creative Commons license and your intended use is not permitted by statutory regulation or exceeds the permitted use, you will need to obtain permission directly from the copyright holder.

The Present: Best Practices and Challenges in AI Ethics Education

AI Ethics in Higher Education: Research Experiences from Practical Development and Deployment of AI Systems

Joyce Nakatumba-Nabende, Conrad Suuna, and Engineer Bainomugisha

1 Introduction

Artificial Intelligence (AI) offers tangible benefits in several application domains like disease diagnosis in health (Muyama et al. 2021; Mahmood et al. 2021), crop disease diagnosis in agriculture (Brahimi et al. 2017; Owomugisha and Mwebaze 2016; Mbelwa et al. 2021) transport and infrastructure (Floyd 2020), environmental monitoring (Coker et al. 2021), and natural language processing (Sefara et al. 2021; Adelani et al. 2021; Nabende et al. 2021; Kabiito and Nakatumba-Nabende 2021). Increasing access to large datasets, improvements in AI models, and accessibility to computational resources have led to growth in the area of AI and particularly machine learning (ML). The growing use of machine learning, in turn, has led to discussions and concerns around ethical aspects. One central ethical concern is about the data used for training machine learning models. For example, an AI-judged beauty context showed that it was biased in the selection of its winners because the model was trained on data that had involved individuals with light-skin tones compared to darker skin tones (Pearson 2016). When an ML algorithm is trained on a dataset that has underlying biases, it can make poor predictions on the underrepresented population. Moreover, if algorithms trained on biased data sets are adapted and used in real-life settings they can exacerbate the discrepancies observed in the data (Liu et al. 2019). Therefore, ethical aspects must be taken into consideration at all stages of building and deploying AI systems.

J. Nakatumba-Nabende (✉) · C. Suuna · E. Bainomugisha
Department of Computer Science, School of Computing and Informatics Technology, Makerere University, Kampala, Uganda
e-mail: joyce.nabende@mak.ac.ug

C. Suuna
e-mail: conrad.suuna@students.mak.ac.ug

E. Bainomugisha
e-mail: baino@mak.ac.ug

In African Universities, three approaches are being taken to grow the AI and data science education and research ecosystem. This has been through the establishment of AI-related data science degree programs (Butcher et al. 2021), setting up AI research labs and centers of excellence, and implementation of practical AI projects. The growing potential of AI has resulted in the establishment of new or strengthening existing university programs in the areas of machine learning, artificial intelligence, bioinformatics, and data science. This is expected to enhance the development of local capacities in AI and data science across the continent. The research labs have been set up within universities and they use AI and machine learning to solve multidisciplinary and practical challenges across several domains in Africa (Makerere Artificial Intelligence Lab 2021; Research Groups—Wits University 2021; Home | CAIR, 2021; Ciira Wa Maina's Homepage 2021; Data Science for Social Impact Research Group—Home 2021). The research labs enable the implementation of practical AI case studies. This provides opportunities for the integration of AI ethics and responsible AI approaches into the educational space. In this paper, we follow these approaches to build a case on the integration of ethical AI around research, innovation, and capacity building. An ethical AI ecosystem should be spearheaded by educators and researchers within the higher institutions of learning. The education sector at universities has the potential to influence students who eventually interact with data collection, model development, and eventual AI system deployment. This is also referred to as the data-to-impact pipeline that is necessary for creating AI solutions and systems (Nakatumba-Nabende 2021). The research labs help to bridge the current gap around the integration of AI ethics in education from a practical research perspective.

In a recent survey by UNESCO, one of the main recommendations for capacity building in organisations to address ethical challenges was to develop educational programs that include AI ethics across different levels in educational institutions development in Africa (Sibal and Neupane n.d.). To fill this gap, this paper presents results from selected universities in Africa to understand the state of AI ethics in graduate programs and experiences in the practical AI systems implemented by AI research labs at these universities. Specifically, we address two research questions:

RQ1: *What is the state of AI ethics in computer science programs at African Universities?*

RQ2: *What are AI ethics issues, lessons, and best practices arising from the practical AI systems implemented by the AI research labs on the continent?*

Our results show that AI ethics is embedded in traditional courses such as research methods, although specific AI ethics courses are also emerging. There is a growing trend of the establishment of AI degree programs and research labs in African higher educational institutions. AI labs are playing a pivotal role in developing relevant curricula and content to support AI ethics research and training. Research work in AI ethics is minimal across the institutions and this is attributed to the growing capacity specifically in the AI ethics field.

The rest of the chapter is structured as follows. In Sect. 2, we detail the topic of AI, AI ethics, the state of AI education, and research in Africa. Section 3 describes the research methodology that we used. Section 4 discusses the results and Sect. 5 concludes the paper.

2 Background

2.1 Ethical Artificial Intelligence

AI technologies are being encountered in several areas of our day-to-day life (Yu et al. 2018). The term AI is frequently used to classify systems that possess characteristics such as learning from experience, discovering meaning, and have the ability to reason (Builtin 2021). Ethical AI speaks to a moral compass that enables people to make ethical decisions during the development and deployment of AI models. This area is now a major focus around the design, development and deployment of AI systems.

There has been growth in the formulation of guidelines, frameworks, consultations around ethical AI from several stakeholders including academia, non-governmental organizations, industry, governments, and international bodies. The Montréal Declaration for Responsible Development of Artificial Intelligence was drafted from an academic perspective and was formed out of a forum on the socially responsible development of AI (Universite de Montreal 2018). Several companies in the industry have also come up with their specific AI ethical principles, for example, Deepmind Ethics and Society Principles (DeepMind 2021), Microsoft AI Principles (Microsoft 2021), and Google AI principles (Google 2021), OECD's Recommendation of the Council on Artificial Intelligence (OECD 2021), and AI4People ethical framework (Floridi et al. 2018). As digitalisation is on the increase on the African continent, a number of African countries are also coming with data protection and privacy acts. Work in AI ethics is also fostered by conferences for example the ACM Conference on Fairness, Accountability, and Transparency (FAccT) that brings together academics and industry to discuss issues around AI fairness, accountability, and transparency. The idea is that we can be able to consider these existing AI ethical frameworks as a basis and use them as a baseline to highlight what applies to the African context.

2.2 AI Ethics Education

Several studies by academia, government, and industry have emphasized the need for developing ethical AI education among key players in the AI ecosystem including, developers, government agencies, users, NGOs, and industry (Taylor and Deb 2021; Raji et al. 2021). AI ethics education should be an important component of AI education at universities if we are to produce ethically responsible AI practitioners. As highlighted in (Raji et al. 2021), how AI ethics is taught is a reflection on how AI practitioners are trained and it shows how academia speaks to practice. This implies that the delivery of AI ethics education at universities is important to ensure it does what it is supposed to do. The suitability of African universities as platforms to address AI ethics education is underwritten by their unique position as conveners, trainers, and mentors of youthful talent, which is more amenable to transformation into future AI developers and decision-makers. Universities are also well networked with governments and private industry, which provide pathways for applied engagement of AI trainees and easier policy uptake of research products.

As shown in Fig. 1, AI ethics education in African universities can be approached from two perspectives. The first approach is through curriculum design and formal instruction in AI ethics where the focus can also draw heavily on existing AI ethical frameworks, guidelines, and principles. Secondly, the formal instruction of AI ethics should be approached from AI research labs' perspectives. These are research labs that are undertaking multidisciplinary AI research projects and they provide practical examples of approaches to AI ethics (Raji et al. 2021). The research labs present an opportunity to emphasize the documentation of the implementation of practical AI local case studies and practical experiences of AI ethics in the African continent. This is because the research labs can also act as a reference and inform AI ethics education. AI research labs should be multidisciplinary and provide a collaborative approach across several disciplines that are critical for interdisciplinary thinking (Kim 2019). This introduces the experience that is required for example through the use of real-world image datasets, for example in healthcare that can greatly foster students to think about aspects of informed consent, privacy, confidentiality, safety, transparency, bias, legal issues even before the AI model development process (Borenstein and Howard 2021; Rigby 2019; Katznelson and Gerke 2021).

Attempts have been made to combine experiences from practical AI projects into the teaching of AI programs for example through a technical curriculum (Williams

Fig. 1 Key ingredients of AI ethics education in African universities

et al. 2020; Burton et al. 2017). However, this is not sufficient and we propose that AI ethics education should be incorporated within the entire AI curriculum that all computer science university students have to follow. This should be done in a case study-based approach as templates for students to practically think about and experience the AI ethical aspects (Burton et al. 2017).

3 Methodology

The study aims to understand how AI research labs and practical research projects are informing AI ethics teaching and education in African Universities. In this section, we describe the methodology and processes used to answer the research questions (**RQ1** and **RQ2**) and derive the results presented in this paper. We employ a blend of expert interviews and case study analysis of the research labs. We received feedback from experts and faculty from 12 Universities and 6 African countries based on a survey in Appendix One. The country distribution includes East Africa (Uganda, Kenya, and Tanzania), Southern Africa (South Africa), and Western Africa (Nigeria and Senegal). Figure 2 shows the distribution of the countries selected representing three African regions.

The respondents included senior faculty, research lab heads, and researchers. A survey was developed to gather feedback from universities and research labs. Institutions include Busitema University, Meru University of Science and Technology, Makerere University, Dedan Kimathi University of Technology, Mbarara University of Science and Technology, Central University of Technology—Free State, Muhimbili University, University Alioune Diop of Bambey, Jaramogi Oginga Odinga University of Science and Technology, Nelson Mandela African Institution of Science and Technology, Federal University Oye Ekiti and the University of Port-Harcourt.

The survey questionnaire consisted of closed and open questions and covered two categories of AI ethics education and research. The respondents were identified through the analysis of institutions that have participated actively in the Africa data science communities such as Data Science Africa (DSA) (Data Science Africa 2021) since its inception in 2013 as well as emerging in-country networks such as the DSA Ugandan chapter (DSA Uganda 2021). The survey was complemented by the authors' knowledge and experience accumulated over the years from designing AI curriculum and involvement in undergraduate and graduate education, implementation and deployment of practical AI systems in Africa, supervision of graduate research and leadership of Computer Science departments and AI research labs. We undertook a document review and analysis of the work carried out in the research labs in the educational institutions and selected case studies of practical implementation of AI systems in the research labs. The case studies considered as part of this research are summarised in Table 1.

Fig. 2 Country distribution of the selected Universities and AI research labs

We analyzed the data from the universities and research labs to derive and form the common themes. The themes were categorised and assigned to the two research questions i.e.:

RQ1: *What is the state of AI ethics in computer science programs at African Universities?* and
RQ2: *What are AI ethics issues, lessons, and best practices arising from the practical AI systems implemented by the AI research labs on the continent?*

Table 1 Mapping of the case studies considered for AI ethics at African Universities

Case study at AI research labs and Universities	What the case study represents
Makerere AI Lab—mCrops project[a]	Practical project implementation of AI for building crop disease diagnosis models for agriculture in Uganda (Owomugisha and Mwebaze 2016)
Makerere AI Lab—AirQo project[b]	Practical implementation of AI for environment monitoring, modeling, and analysis in Uganda (Coker et al. 2021)
Makerere AI Lab—rCrops project[c]	Practical implementation of AI for building speech recognition models based on radio streams in Uganda (Akera et al. 2019)
Dedan Kimathi University of Technology	Practical implementation of the use of the internet of things (IoT) for water quality monitoring (Mokua et al. 2021)
Marconi Machine Learning Lab[d]	Practical project implementation of building AI for cervical cancer diagnosis in Uganda and AI systems for passion fruit disease identification (Katumba et al. 2020)
Makerere AI Lab—Ocula project[e]	Practical project implementation of building AI for microscopy diseases: malaria, tuberculosis, and intestinal worms in Uganda (Muyama et al. 2021; Quinn et al. 2016)
Nelson Mandela African Institute of Science and Technology	Practical project implementation of building AI for poultry diseases diagnostics and bioinformatics methods for small and medium-scale poultry farmers in Tanzania (Mbelwa et al. 2021)
Muhimbili University[f]	Adopting Ada (an artificial intelligence AI-system) to support medical decision making during the process of diagnosis in Tanzania

[a] mCrops project. http://34.242.164.142/mcrops/
[b] AirQo. https://airqo.africa
[c] https://air.ug/projects/#thumb9
[d] https://ml.netlabsug.org
[e] https://air.ug/microscopy/
[f] https://drp.muhas.ac.tz/Research

4 Results and Discussion

In this section, we present results from the analysis and provide a discussion of the lessons and emerging issues to help inform academicians and researchers of AI ethics at African institutions of higher learning. Table 2 provides a summary of the lessons and emerging issues from the analysis. Lessons L1-4 are the lessons and issues that emerged from the AI ethics education from the selected African universities, while

Table 2 Lessons and emerging issues of teaching AI Ethics in higher education in Africa

Theme	Lessons and emerging issues
AI ethics education in African Universities	**L1**: AI ethics is embedded in traditional research methods, although specific courses are emerging
	L2: AI ethics is offered across undergraduate and postgraduate levels at the University
	L3: There is the use of global AI ethics frameworks with some glocalisation
	L4: Institutional AI ethics local capacity is still developing
Role of AI research labs and practical projects in AI ethics education at African Universities	**L5**: African Universities are establishing AI labs
	L6: Minimal AI ethics-specific research themes
	L7: AI labs are providing relevant content for curricula and serve as a vehicle for experiential learning for AI ethics
	L8: AI labs are playing a critical role in promoting AI ethics research and training

L5-8 presents the results on how AI research labs and practical project implementations are shaping the landscape of teaching AI ethics in University programs as well as graduate research. AI ethics in education is an emerging topic, therefore, these lessons are not necessarily conclusive. Moreover, the teaching of AI ethics is also dependent on changing policy and regulatory landscape at national and internal levels. For example, African governments are formulating policies, strategies, and regulations that could have implications on the priority of AI ethics in education and practice, for example, the Data Protection and Privacy Act exists in Uganda (The Data Protection and Privacy Act 2019) and Kenya (The Data Protection Act 2019).

4.1 AI Ethics Education in African Universities

Under this theme, we set out to answer the research question "*RQ1: What is the state of AI ethics in computer science programs at African Universities?*" to understand the level of awareness of AI ethics among University degree programs, approaches that are employed by African Universities to teach AI ethics at Universities and any emerging issues. AI as a field where AI ethics fall is still developing across the selected African institutions. There are emerging AI-specific courses in about half of the institutions surveyed. Makerere University in Uganda has revised its Master's in Computer Science programme to include a specialised track on AI and Data Science (Department of Computer Science 2021).

We found that AI ethics is embedded in traditional research methods courses, although specific short courses and modules are emerging (**L1**), other institutions are in the process of revising their curricula and integrating AI ethics courses. From the selected institutions 40% of the respondents indicated that AI ethics is embedded in research methods courses, while in other cases teaching of AI ethics is considered as modules in AI and machine learning courses such as Machine Learning, Artificial Intelligence, Data Mining, and Data Processing. Designing curricula to accommodate various courses is often challenging and therefore the approach of blending ethics across is sometimes considered an optimal approach given its cross-cutting nature. Teaching and delivery of AI ethics courses are largely theoretical with minimal practical class projects. Topics covered include algorithmic bias and fairness, gender, explainability, security and privacy, and data ownership and protection. In some institutions, standard curricula are complemented by specialised modules, professional courses, reading clubs, institutional research ethics committees, seminars, and conferences. For example, past editions of the Data Science Africa workshop, whose audience is largely African University students and faculty, have featured talks and panel discussions on Ethics in AI with topics on ethical challenges in health, security aspects for data engineering. Moreover, Makerere University has developed Open AI Training modules with a specialized topic on the identification and elimination of biases in AI training data.[1]

AI ethics is offered across undergraduate and postgraduate levels in the University (**L2**) with the majority of the institutions teaching AI ethics at the Bachelor's degree level, followed by the Master's programs, and professional short courses and modules. Institutional AI ethics local capacity is still developing (**L4**) at many African universities, with only a few faculty involved in AI research in general and minimal graduate research in AI ethics (20%). This suggests that AI ethics is considered as a crosscutting concern than a standalone research topic or theme for research. There is the use of global AI Ethics Frameworks with some glocalisation (**L3**), for teaching and implementation of practical AI research projects. Faculty reported the use of several global AI ethical frameworks as discussed in Sect. 2, for example, AI Now Reports, Microsoft AI principles, DeepMind Ethics and Society Principles, etc. The use of AI ethical frameworks during AI project development and deployment was low at 10% of the respondents. This suggests a lack of awareness of global AI ethics frameworks or limited capacity in considering ethical issues. In the future, it would be interesting to undertake a detailed review of the fit of global AI ethical frameworks for the AI projects in the African context and to explore any glocalisation opportunities therein.

---

[1] https://github.com/AI-Lab-Makerere/courses-on-open-and-unbiasedAI-training-data.

4.2 Role of AI Research Labs and Practical Projects in AI Ethics Education at African Universities

Here we present the emerging lessons and issues under the research question "What are AI ethics issues, lessons and best practices arising from the practical AI systems implemented by the AI research labs on the continent?". The purpose of this research question was to find out the role of research labs in AI ethics education and research in African universities and any emerging ethical issues from the implementation of the practical AI projects in the African context. African Universities are establishing AI labs and centers to propel AI research and education on the continent (**L5**), with 68% confirming the existence of an AI research lab at their institution. The major application domains of focus for the research labs include Health (75%), Agriculture (50%), and Environment (42%) indicating the priority of African institutions to undertake AI research that addresses key development challenges facing the continent (Fig. 3). These themes are consistent with those identified in previous studies on the role of AI on social impact in emerging economies (Tomašev et al. 2020). The major technical sub-themes across the selected African institutions and countries include Computer Vision, Machine Learning, Artificial Intelligence, Robotics, Natural Language Processing, Mobile Computing, the Internet-of-Things, and Human-Computer Interaction. There are minimal AI ethics-specific research themes in the AI research labs (**L6**) and graduate research in AI ethics is still in its infancy. In some institutions, AI research labs are establishing sub-groups focussing on AI ethics. However, AI in graduate research is still low with only 20% of the faculty surveyed indicating that their research labs have graduate students researching in the area of AI ethics. No single institution reported an AI ethics research paper. This finding shows a gap in raising the profile of AI ethics research. Some institutions attributed this to the lack of funding and lack of local capacity to research in the area.

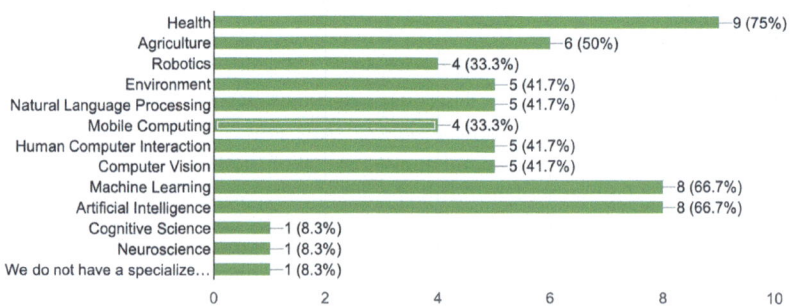

Fig. 3 Major focus areas and application domains of AI research labs

Table 3 AI ethics issues identified in practical projects implemented by the AI labs

Research focus	AI ethical considerations
AI in health	Informed consent, privacy, confidentiality, safety, transparency, bias, explainability, algorithmic fairness, explicability
AI in agriculture	Transparency, inclusion, security, privacy, accuracy, data ownership, explainability, explicability
Natural language processing	Bias (gender, racial), exclusion, discrimination, diversity, algorithmic fairness, transparency, explicability
AI in environment	Security and data privacy, economic and political harm, misuse, algorithmic fairness and biases, accuracy, explainability

Despite the minimal AI ethics research topics, AI research labs are providing relevant content for AI ethics curricula and serving as an essential vehicle for experiential learning (**L7**). Development and delivery of AI ethics curricula on the African continent can be at risk of replicating content taught elsewhere without much consideration of the relevance and fit to the unique AI ethics issues for the continent. AI research labs are involved in the implementation of AI projects and can use that experience to enrich AI ethics curricula with real-world examples from the development and deployment of AI systems. Take, for example, the AI lab at Makerere University first started a specialised track in Computer Vision in 2009 and recently leveraged the practical experience in developing and deploying local AI systems to improve the curricula and develop relevant content. Further, AI labs are critical in contributing to relevant graduate education and research in AI ethics (**L8**). African in general lacks sufficient local case studies to support the training of AI ethics and AI topics. Therefore documentation of AI ethics arising from local AI practical projects that are being implemented at the labs is critical in the quality of AI ethics teaching and delivery. Table 3 shows an overview of the AI ethical issues derived from the example practical projects implemented by the AI research labs.

The institutions surveyed employ different approaches to complement AI training and research including research seminars especially for graduate students, mentorship, practical AI ethics research topics, internships, and student job opportunities. Although AI labs reported having experienced AI ethics issues in research project implementation, the documentation of the issues arising from the practice is still lacking. This potential area for future work is a step towards developing AI ethics education and research in Africa.

5 Conclusion, Limitations, and Recommendations

This paper presents the state of AI ethics in education at African Universities and the critical role AI research labs play to support AI ethics teaching and education. Although the number of use cases and universities is limited, we hope that the results of this study are important in providing a framework for the use of AI research carried out in enhancing the teaching of AI ethics in other African universities. The field of AI ethics and in general AI and machine learning are emerging across African Universities. The AI research labs can help to demystify the potential and applicability of AI and machine learning in the African setting, thereby leading to increased interest in the field for students, staff, and the industry. Previously the lack of local AI and machine learning projects led to the perception that AI and machine learning are only applicable to developed countries and teaching of topics such as AI ethics was largely theoretical. This is also applicable to the teaching of AI ethics without local examples that students and staff can connect with. We recommend that African Universities undertake the following steps to improve the teaching of AI ethics (1) Development of AI ethics training programs, curricula, courses, and relevant content informed by practical *local* experiences from AI research labs. (2) Documentation of AI ethical issues in local case studies practical projects and making these accessible to students and faculty (3) Undertaking AI ethics-specific research in the research labs as means to grow local capacity. (4) *Glocalisation* of the existing AI ethics frameworks and using the resulting customised frameworks in teaching and research project implementation. These should be applicable to the arising aspects of ethical AI within the African context.

Acknowledgements The authors would like to thank all AI researchers and faculty from institutions who provided feedback and shared their experiences on the state and education of AI ethics in their institutions. This work was carried out with the aid of a grant from the International Development Research Centre Canada, and the Swedish International Development Cooperation Agency, and Google.org.

Appendix 1: Survey Questions

1. Your Name
2. Email Address
3. Country of residence
4. University/Institution
5. Does your institution offer any specific courses on AI ethics?

    - Yes
    - No

6. Under what courses are AI ethics taught in your institution (e.g., Machine Learning, Artificial Intelligence, Data Science, Research Methods)?
7. At what level are the AI ethics courses offered in your institution?

    - Bachelors
    - Masters
    - Ph.D.
    - Short courses

8. How are AI ethical issues being delivered in teaching at your institution?
   - Theoretical classes
   - Practical class projects
   - Other...
9. What other ways is AI ethics taught/delivered in your institution (if any)?
10. What guidelines/frameworks are being used for teaching AI ethics in your institution?
11. Do you have any graduate students undertaking ethics in AI as a research topic/focus?
    - Yes
    - No
12. What example research topics are being undertaken by the student(s)?
13. If AI ethics is not being taught to students, what effort is being made to make students aware of AI ethics?
14. What efforts are being put in place, through teachings/ practices to build local capacity in AI ethics?
15. Does your institution have AI or ML Research labs?
    - Yes
    - No
16. Is AI ethics one of the research focus areas in your institutional labs?
    - Yes
    - No
17. What is the research focus/application domain of AI labs in your institution?
    - Health
    - Agriculture
    - Robotics
    - Environment
    - Natural Language Processing
    - Mobile Computing
    - Human-Computer Interaction
    - Computer Vision
    - Machine Learning
    - Artificial Intelligence
    - Cognitive Learning
    - Other...
18. How is the research focus/work being done in your institutional lab used to strengthen the teaching and delivery of AI ethical courses?
19. Describe any AI ethics issues that you have experienced in your research project implementation.

20. How are AI ethical issues being addressed in the research or in the practical development of the AI applications at your institution?
21. How many people are involved in the different AI research areas at your institutional labs?

    - Below 30
    - 30–60
    - Above 60

22. Do you use any AI ethics guidelines/frameworks during system development and deployment in your institutional labs?

    - Yes
    - No

23. Please specify any frameworks, if any, being used in the development and deployment of the systems.
24. Are there any ethical issues that emerge from the AI systems being developed in the institutional labs?

    - Yes
    - No

25. How are they handled?
26. Do you have any published works in AI ethics?

    - Yes
    - No

27. Provide links to the published work.

References

Adelani, D.I., J. Abbott, G. Neubig, D. D'souza, J. Kreutzer, C. Lignos, C. Palen-Michel, H. Buzaaba, S. Rijhwani, S. Ruder, S. Mayhew, I.A. Azime, S.H. Muhammad, C.C. Emezue, J. Nakatumba-Nabende, P. Ogayo, A. Anuoluwapo, C. Gitau, and D. Mbaye, et al. 2021. MasakhaNER: Named Entity Recognition for African Languages. *Transactions of the Association for Computational Linguistics* 9: 1116–1131. https://doi.org/10.1162/tacl_a_00416.

Akera, B., Nakatumba-Nabende, J., Mukiibi, J., Hussein, A., Baleeta, N., Sendiwala, D., and Nalwooga, S. (2019). *Keyword Spotter Model for Crop Pest and Disease Monitoring from Community Radio Data.* 33rd Conference on Neural Information Processing Systems (NeurIPS 2019) Machine Learning for Developing World (ML4D).

Borenstein, J., and A. Howard. 2021. Emerging Challenges in AI and the Need for AI Ethics Education. *AI and Ethics* 1 (1): 61–65. https://doi.org/10.1007/s43681-020-00002-7.

Brahimi, M., K. Boukhalfa, and A. Moussaoui. 2017. Deep Learning for Tomato Diseases: Classification and Symptoms Visualization. *Applied Artificial Intelligence* 31 (4): 299–315. https://doi.org/10.1080/08839514.2017.1315516.

Builtin. (2021). *What is Artificial Intelligence? How Does AI Work?* https://builtin.com/artificial-intelligence.

Burton, E., J. Goldsmith, S. Koenig, B. Kuipers, N. Mattei, and T. Walsh. 2017. Ethical Considerations in Artificial Intelligence Courses. *AI Magazine* 38 (2): 22–34. https://doi.org/10.1609/aimag.v38i2.2731.

Butcher, N., Wilson-Strydom, M., and Baijnath, M. 2021. *Artificial Intelligence Capacity in Sub-Saharan Africa: Compendium Report*. https://idl-bnc-idrc.dspacedirect.org/handle/10625/59999.

Ciira wa Maina's Homepage. 2021. http://ciirawamaina.com/projects.html.

Coker, E.S., A.K. Amegah, E. Mwebaze, J. Ssematimba, and E. Bainomugisha. 2021. A Land use Regression Model Using Machine Learning and Locally Developed Low Cost Particulate Matter Sensors in Uganda. *Environmental Research* 199: 111352. https://doi.org/10.1016/j.envres.2021.111352.

Data Science Africa. 2021. http://www.datascienceafrica.org/.

Data Science for Social Impact Research Group—Home. 2021. https://dsfsi.github.io/.

DeepMind. (2021). *Ethics & Society Team*. Deepmind. /about/ethics-and-society

Department of Computer Science. 2021. *Makerere University Master of Computer Science*. https://cs.mak.ac.ug/curriculum/masters.

DSA Uganda. 2021. http://www.datascienceafrica.org/dsaUganda/.

Floridi, L., J. Cowls, M. Beltrametti, R. Chatila, P. Chazerand, V. Dignum, C. Luetge, R. Madelin, U. Pagallo, F. Rossi, B. Schafer, P. Valcke, and E. Vayena. 2018. AI4People—An Ethical Framework for a Good AI Society: Opportunities, Risks, Principles, and Recommendations. *Minds and Machines* 28 (4): 689–707. https://doi.org/10.1007/s11023-018-9482-5.

Floyd, R. 2020. *ACET Uses Artificial Intelligence to Predict Future African Infrastructure Needs*. https://acetforafrica.org/highlights/acet-uses-artificial-intelligence-to-predict-future-african-infrastructure-needs/.

Google. 2021. *Google AI Principles*. Google AI. https://ai.google/principles/.

Home | CAIR. 2021. https://www.cair.za.net/.

Kabiito, D., and J. Nakatumba-Nabende. 2021. Targeted Aspect-Based Sentiment Analysis for Ugandan Telecom Reviews from Twitter. In *Advances in Artificial Intelligence and Applied Cognitive Computing*, eds. H.R. Arabnia, K. Ferens, D. de la Fuente, E.B. Kozerenko, J.A. Olivas Varela, and F.G. Tinetti, 311–322. Springer International Publishing.

Katumba, A., M. Bomera, C. Mwikirize, G. Namulondo, M.G. Ajero, Ramathani, I., Nakayima, O., Nakabonge, G., Okello, D., & Serugunda, J. 2020. A Deep Learning-based Detector for Brown Spot Disease in Passion Fruit Plant Leaves. http://arxiv.org/abs/2007.14103.

Katznelson, G., and S. Gerke 2021. The need for health AI ethics in medical school education. *Advances in Health Sciences Education : Theory and Practice*. https://doi.org/10.1007/s10459-021-10040-3.

Kim, B. 2019. AI and Creating the First Multidisciplinary AI Lab. *Library Technology Reports*, 6.

Liu, T., A. Venkatachalam, P. Sanjay Bongale, and C. Homan. 2019. Learning to Predict Population-Level Label Distributions. In *Companion Proceedings of the 2019 World Wide Web Conference*, 1111–1120. https://doi.org/10.1145/3308560.3317082.

Mahmood, H., M. Shaban, N. Rajpoot, and S.A. Khurram. 2021. Artificial Intelligence-Based Methods in Head and Neck Cancer Diagnosis: An Overview. *British Journal of Cancer*. https://doi.org/10.1038/s41416-021-01386-x.

Makerere Artificial Intelligence Lab. (2021). https://air.ug/

Mbelwa, H., J. Mbelwa, and D. Machuve. 2021. Deep Convolutional Neural Network for Chicken Diseases Detection. *International Journal of Advanced Computer Science and Applications* 12 (2): 759–765.

Microsoft. 2021. *Responsible AI principles from Microsoft*. Microsoft. https://www.microsoft.com/en-us/ai/responsible-ai.

Mokua, Nanshon, Ciira Maina, and Henry Kiragi. 2021. Anomaly Detection for Raw Water Quality—A Comparative Analysis of the Local Outlier Factor Algorithm and the Random Forest Algorithms. *International Journal of Computer Applications* 174 (26): 49–54.

Muyama, L., J. Nakatumba-Nabende, and D. Mudali. 2021. *Automated Detection of Tuberculosis from Sputum Smear Microscopic Images Using Transfer Learning Techniques.* https://link.springer.com/chapter/10.1007/978-3-030-49342-4_6.

Nabende, P., D. Kabiito, C. Babirye, H. Tusiime, and J. Nakatumba-Nabende. 2021. Misinformation detection in Luganda-English code-mixed social media text. In *Proceedings of the 2021 African NLP Workshop.* https://arxiv.org/abs/2104.00124.

Nakatumba-Nabende, J. 2021. Leveraging AI. *Feminist AI.* https://feministai.pubpub.org/pub/leveraging-ai.

OECD. (2021). *OECD Legal Instruments.* https://legalinstruments.oecd.org/en/instruments/OECD-LEGAL-0449

Owomugisha, G., and E. Mwebaze. 2016. Machine Learning for Plant Disease Incidence and Severity Measurements from Leaf Images. In *2016 15th IEEE International Conference on Machine Learning and Applications (ICMLA),* 158–163. https://doi.org/10.1109/ICMLA.2016.0034.

Pearson, J. 2016. *Why An AI-Judged Beauty Contest Picked Nearly All White Winners.* https://www.vice.com/en/article/78k7de/why-an-ai-judged-beauty-contest-picked-nearly-all-white-winners.

Quinn, J.A., R. Nakasi, P.K.B. Mugagga, P. Byanyima, W. Lubega, and A. Andama, A. 2016. Deep Convolutional Neural Networks for Microscopy-Based Point of Care Diagnostics. In *Proceedings of the 1st Machine Learning for Healthcare Conference,* vol. 56, eds. F. Doshi-Velez, J. Fackler, D. Kale, B. Wallace, and J. Wiens, 271–281. PMLR. https://proceedings.mlr.press/v56/Quinn16.html.

Raji, I.D., M.K. Scheuerman, and R. Amironesei. 2021. You Can't Sit With Us: Exclusionary Pedagogy in AI Ethics Education. In *Proceedings of the 2021 ACM Conference on Fairness, Accountability, and Transparency,* 515–525. https://doi.org/10.1145/3442188.3445914.

Research Groups—Wits University. 2021. https://www.wits.ac.za/csam/research/research-groups/.

Rigby, M.J. 2019. Ethical Dimensions of Using Artificial Intelligence in Health Care. *AMA Journal of Ethics* 21 (2): 121–124. https://doi.org/10.1001/amajethics.2019.121.

Sefara, T.J., S.G. Zwane, N. Gama, H. Sibisi, P.N. Senoamadi, and V. Marivate. 2021. Transformer-based Machine Translation for Low-resourced Languages embedded with Language Identification. In *2021 Conference on Information Communications Technology and Society (ICTAS),* 127–132. https://doi.org/10.1109/ICTAS50802.2021.9394996.

Sibal, P., and B. Neupane. n.d. *Artificial Intelligence Needs Assessment Survey in Africa—UNESCO Digital Library.* https://unesdoc.unesco.org/ark:/48223/pf0000375322. Accessed 30 May 2021.

Taylor, G., and D. Deb. 2021. Teaching AI Ethics in a Flipped Classroom. *Journal of Computing Sciences in Colleges* 36 (5): 67–76.

The Data Protection Act. 2019. http://kenyalaw.org/kl/fileadmin/pdfdownloads/Acts/2019/TheDataProtectionAct__No24of2019.pdf.

The Data Protection and Privacy Act. 2019. https://ict.go.ug/wp-content/uploads/2019/03/Data-Protection-and-Privacy-Act-2019.pdf.

Tomašev, N., J. Cornebise, F. Hutter, S. Mohamed, A. Picciariello, B. Connelly, D.C.M. Belgrave, D. Ezer, F.C. van der Haert, F. Mugisha, G. Abila, H. Arai, H. Almiraat, J. Proskurnia, K. Snyder, M. Otake-Matsuura, M. Othman, T. Glasmachers, W. de Wever, et al. 2020. AI for Social Good: Unlocking the Opportunity for Positive Impact. *Nature Communications* 11 (1): 2468. https://doi.org/10.1038/s41467-020-15871-z.

Universite de Montreal. 2018. *Montréal Declaration of Responsible AI: 2018 Overview of International Recommendations for AI Ethics.* Respaideclaration. https://www.montrealdeclaration-responsibleai.com/reports-of-montreal-declaration.

Williams, T., Q. Zhu, and D. Grollman. 2020. An Experimental Ethics Approach to Robot Ethics Education. In *Proceedings of the AAAI Conference on Artificial Intelligence.* https://ojs.aaai.org/index.php/AAAI/article/view/7067.

Yu, H., Z. Shen, C. Miao, C. Leung, V.R. Lesser, and Q. Yang. 2018. Building Ethics into Artificial Intelligence. http://arxiv.org/abs/1812.02953.

Open Access This chapter is licensed under the terms of the Creative Commons Attribution 4.0 International License (http://creativecommons.org/licenses/by/4.0/), which permits use, sharing, adaptation, distribution and reproduction in any medium or format, as long as you give appropriate credit to the original author(s) and the source, provide a link to the Creative Commons license and indicate if changes were made.

The images or other third party material in this chapter are included in the chapter's Creative Commons license, unless indicated otherwise in a credit line to the material. If material is not included in the chapter's Creative Commons license and your intended use is not permitted by statutory regulation or exceeds the permitted use, you will need to obtain permission directly from the copyright holder.

Challenges of Integrating AI Ethics into Higher Education Curricula in West Africa: Nigerian Universities Narrative

Laeticia N. Onyejegbu

Artificial intelligence (AI) is becoming more pervasive and intriguing. This is because AI is improving our lives by doing much of the difficult work for us, such as driving our automobiles, performing medical tasks, accounting tasks, and a variety of other tasks. It can also acquire new knowledge. It is a non-human machine that can be used to achieve a difficult goal. Although AI has demonstrable benefits, the collection, use, and misuse of data required to train and feed AI, as well as the algorithm itself, may expose people to risks they are not aware of (Borenstein and Howard 2021). This calls for the need to build next generation of AI technologies that can make a difference by integrating Ethics in AI. In 2018, the world became really concerned about AI ethics, and that was not because suddenly across borders, across sectors, we became enlightened. It is because for any good AI ethics research, the source and the quality of data used is very important and should be adequate. There are issues of social media, the world is under threat, algorithms may reinforce discrimination and even amplify it. Important questions are being raised since the machine is aiming at replacing humans, could artificial intelligence be harmful to humanity? In response to these issues, more institutions started to focus on AI Ethics. Africa will not be left out. This calls for the need to integrate AI ethics into higher education curricula in Africa. AI Ethics will help to build a human-centric approach, where tomorrow's challenges and citizens' aspirations are considered. We also believe that it will help to safeguard humanity.

Despite warnings from people like Elon Musk about the existential risk AI technology poses to humanity (Vincent 2017), the reality is that it is a useful tool, even in education but it needs human control. AI does not have awareness of itself, nor does it have something called "empathy" which is the fundament of ethics. Despite the clear need to understand how AI affects people around the world, a truly global perspective remains a critical blind spot in the ethics conversation. The United Nations, national

---

L. N. Onyejegbu (✉)
Computer Science Department, Faculty of Computing, University of Port Harcourt, Port Harcourt, Nigeria

legislators and industrial bodies in developed countries are asking these questions and are already acting to protect their constituents from some potentially negative effects of AI, such as algorithmic discrimination and voter manipulation (Gwagwa 2019).

1 AI Ethics

Over the past few years, various measures and initiatives have been put in place to promote ethical development and use of AI technology. But currently, 'ethics' is not being used for artificial intelligence the way it ought to. An AI system will do whatever task it has been ordered to do even if these tasks are unethical, illegal, or lead to adverse outcomes. Ethics is simply defined as "doing the right thing at the intersection of technology innovation and accepted social values" (O'Brien 2020). It is about behaviour and about ways of thinking, especially in situations where the choice made can affect the dignity and wellbeing of others. AI Ethics is about integrating ethical constructs into how organizations develop new technologies. Ethics is not only important in technology (and especially AI), but it should be the foundation of any innovation.

AI will radically transform and disrupt the world, but right ethical choices for AI can make it a force of good for humanity. Until governments, business sector and academics start thinking about bringing codes of ethics into the AI discussion there is no anchor for the AI disruption. There is a need for setting up global AI ethics standards. Codes of ethics for expert bodies have broader national or global context. An international regulatory model is essential for the responsible design, development and deployment of AI (Hashmi 2019).

Figure 1 shows AI Ethics principles which is the framework needed to build ethical AI.

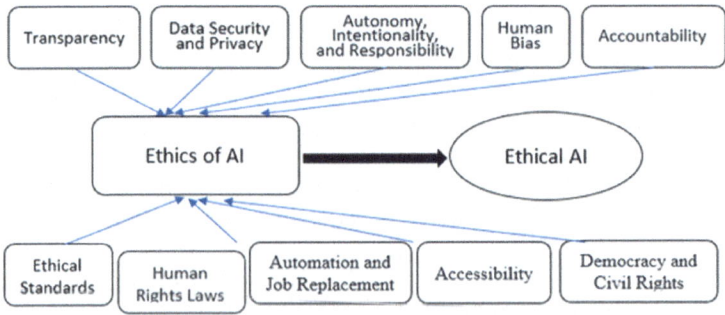

Fig. 1 AI Ethics: Framework of building ethical AI. *Source* https://www.researchgate.net/profile/Keng-Siau-of-building-ethical-AI.ppm

Ethics of AI studies the ethical principles, rules, guidelines, policies, and regulations that are related to AI. Ethical AI is an AI that performs and behaves ethically. One must recognize and understand the potential ethical and moral issues that may be caused by AI to formulate the necessary ethical principles, rules, guidelines, policies, and regulations for AI (i.e., Ethics of AI). With the appropriate Ethics of AI, one can then build AI that exhibits ethical behaviour (i.e., Ethical AI) (Siau and Wang 2020).

Figure 1 establishes the framework for AI ethics listing the factors or principles that needs to be considered in defining the ethics of AI in order to build ethical AI. They include transparency, data security and privacy, autonomy, intentionality and responsibility, Human bias, accountability, ethical standards, human rights laws, automation and job replacement, accessibility, democracy, and civil right. Even though defining the ethics of AI is multifaceted and convoluted, putting the ethics of AI into practice to build ethical AI is not easy. Ethical sensitivity training is required to make good ethical decisions. In theory, AI should be able to recognize ethical issues. If AI can make decisions, how can it be designed and developed for it to be sensitive to ethical issues? Long-term and sustained efforts are needed. Nonetheless, understanding and realizing the importance of developing ethical AI and starting to work on it step by step are positive steps forward. Many institutions, such as Google, IBM, Accenture, Microsoft, and Atomium-EISMD, have started working on building ethical principles to guide the development of AI. Ethical AI should do no harm to humans (Siau and Wang 2020).

Therefore, to ensure AI remains human-centric, companies developing or using AI should promote ethical debates that lead to codes of conduct based on principles that will safely guide humanity.

2 Importance of Ethics in AI Courses

AI does not have awareness of itself, nor does it have something called "empathy" which is the fundamental of ethics. It could be developed with good intentions, but still, draft into something less morally approved. So, ethics is not only important in technology (and especially AI), but it should be the foundation of any innovation (Hoes 2019).

The growing presence of AI calls for its political, economic, and social consideration and, most importantly, ethical implications. It is therefore crucial to lay the groundwork to avoid situations in which machines make decisions that affect individuals in the future, such as creating biases that single out or exclude individuals based on race or gender. Failure to adopt ethical frameworks to address issues that may arise in terms of personal data collection and processing can damage a business' reputation and cause direct and possibly irreparable harm to consumers.

Recognition of the need for ethics education in computer science, information technology, engineering and other related disciplines goes back at least a hundred years, but it has only been since the 1990s that expectations for ethics education have been adopted by accreditation bodies (Furey and Martin 2018). It also raises the need for real and honest dialogue about how we build and adopt these technologies responsibly.

AI Ethics is not currently a course in computer science, engineering, information technology departments in Nigeria federal and state Universities. What all the Universities in Nigeria has in its Benchmark Minimum Academic Standard (BMAS), is AI BMAS. For example, in University of Port Harcourt, AI is not a stand-alone program, but it is a core course, for computer science, and electrical/electronic engineering undergraduate students. The same applies to the graduate (MSc and PhD) computer science and electrical/electronic students. It is not an elective course nor a stand-alone programme. It is a core course.

There is a deep concern about the increasing wide-reaching societal impact of AI approaches. This calls for the academia, to create ethical awareness while teaching AI. They should educate students and the workforce whose jobs are evolving with AI, on how human checks and balances can be enforced on AI machines.

AI systems should be developed and used according to the following rules: respect for human autonomy, prevention of harm, fairness, and explicability. The attention is paid to certain social groups: children, disabled people, and other groups at risk of exclusion. AI may be beneficial, but it comes with risks that are sometimes difficult to predict and identify. This calls for the need to integrate ethics into AI course. For instructors, there is need to develop curriculum that not only prepares students to be artificial intelligence practitioners, but also to understand the moral, ethical, and philosophical impacts that artificial intelligence will have on society. To avoid running the risk of not being ethical, AI technology must be build based on ethics and every outcome of the algorithms used for implementing it, should be understood.

Figure 2 shows a diagrammatic representation of what Ethics in AI means.

From Fig. 2, it is important to include ethics in AI course because it will eliminate or reduce bias, provide trust, the system developed will be transparent. It can be explained and interpreted, it will protect human privacy, and it will be built and used with ethical purpose in mind.

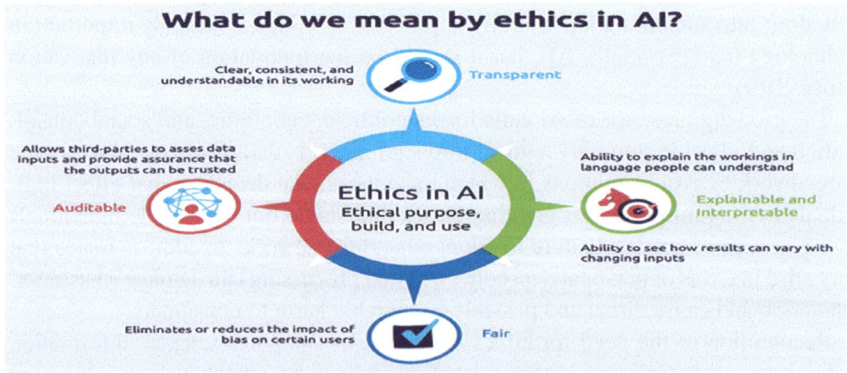

Fig. 2 Ethics in AI. *Source* https://img2.helpnetsecurity.com/posts2019/ethics-ai.jpg

3 The Need to Integrate AI Ethics into Higher Education Curricula

It is vital that there is open, informed dialogue and transparency about the ethical quandaries of AI and education if trust is to be developed in the technology. The teaching profession has a long history of leading public discussion and providing accessible explanations on complex issues which affect students and their families and of grappling with issues of fairness, ethics, duty of care, and accountability in schooling. This makes the teaching profession well equipped, to both use AI technology for good and to ask critical questions regarding when and how machines should guide student learning and decision processes within educational settings, and whose values should be imbued into AI-powered systems (Southgate 2018).

The goal of teaching ethical theory is to better equip students to understand ethical problems by exposing them to multiple modes of thinking and reasoning. This is best accomplished by helping them understand the powers and limits of each approach, rather than trying to demonstrate the superiority of one approach over the other.

Teaching ethics in AI classes is important since AI technologies and their applications raise ethical issues, it makes sense to devote one or more lectures of an introductory AI class (or even a whole course) to them. Students should think about the ethical issues that AI technologies and systems raise, they should learn about ethical theories that provide frameworks that enable them to think about the ethical issues and apply their knowledge to one or more case studies, both to describe what is happening in them and to think about possible solutions to the ethical problems they pose. AI Ethics is a rich topic that should support a full-semester course. As such there is need to integrate AI Ethics as part of computer science and engineering university programs (Eleanor et al. 2020). To effectively integrate AI Ethics into higher education curricula in West Africa, requires collaboration between universities across countries and research institutes. Responsible AI networks in West Africa should be encouraged.

An on-line survey was conducted by the researcher, to find out if universities offer AI ethics as a program. Figure 3 presents the feedback of some selected universities in Africa that offer AI ethics as a program. From the figure, 88.5% of the selected universities, do not offer AI ethics as a program, while 11.5% offer AI ethics as a program.

4 AI Ethics for Africa's Development

Despite the global nature of the ethical implications of artificial intelligence, attention has focused primarily on the US and the EU, with growing awareness of China, especially its increasing AI capabilities, its impact on the Global South and the global geopolitical order. Despite the clear need to understand how AI affects people around the world, a truly global perspective remains a critical blind spot in the

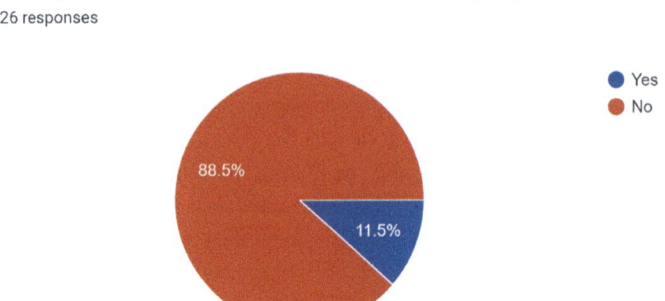

Fig. 3 The percentage of institution in some West Africa and African countries that offer AI ethics as a program

ethics conversation. The United Nations, national legislators and industrial bodies in developed countries are asking these questions and are already acting to protect their constituents from some potentially negative effects of AI, such as: algorithmic discrimination and voter manipulation.

Is Africa included in the processes of the emerging global AI ethics initiatives, including the nascent ones in Africa? And are issues that are relevant to Africa being addressed in such initiatives? (Gwagwa 2019).

West African higher institutions are playing a critical role in growing the AI ecosystems through AI and data science programmes, research labs and AI centres of excellence. These efforts are expected to lead harnessing AI full potential in the economic development of Africa. Although AI holds high potential for the African continent, it also carries along risks and harms that must be considered to achieve responsible and sustainable AI for development. Universities have a critical role in shaping the landscape of AI ethics in Africa. AI ethics can be described as "a set of values, principles, and techniques that employ widely accepted standards of right and wrong to guide moral conduct in the development and use of AI technologies" (Eleanor et al. 2020).

Figure 4 shows a conceptual framework that can provide a solid foundation to address the way socially responsible intelligent AI systems are build. This approach aims to form a set of standards as an ethical blueprint that developers and customers will make use of. For example, ethical laid down laws should be followed; what is AI forbidden to do, is human life rights been considered, and in making regulations is the right AI tools been used (Girard 2020).

Figure 5 shows the graphical feedback of the online survey conducted by the researcher on, the challenges of integrating AI ethics into higher institutions curricula in Africa, from selected African countries. Responses were gotten from some AI experts from different universities while conducting the online survey for this work. From Fig. 5, there are 17 feedbacks from the universities in Nigeria, two from

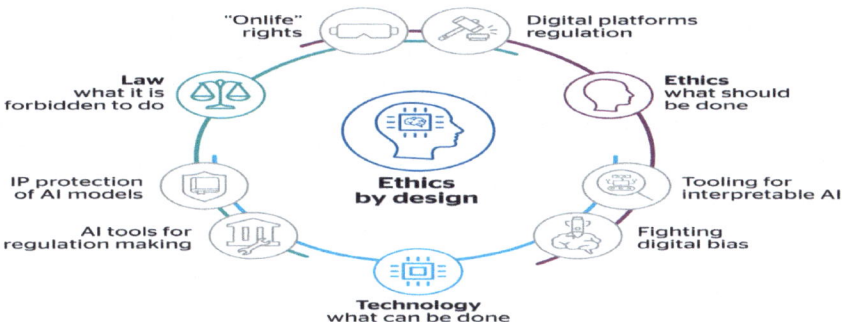

Fig. 4 AI ethics by design. *Source* Girard (2020)

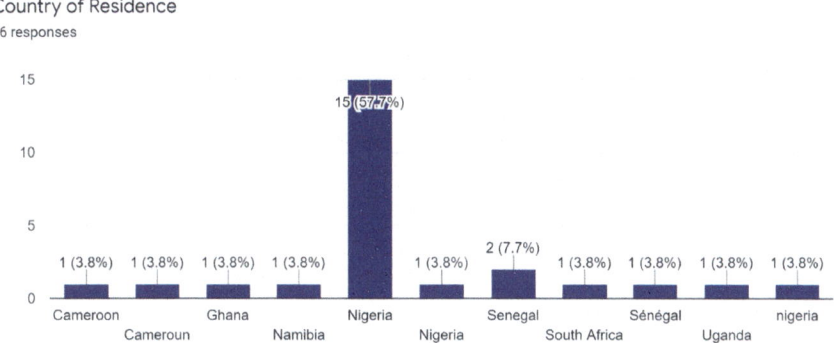

Fig. 5 Survey report from some African countries

Cameroon, one from Ghana, one from Namibia, two from Senegal, one from South Africa, and one from Uganda.

5 Challenges of Integrating AI Ethics into Higher Education Curricula

There are challenges associated with integrating AI ethics into higher education curricula in Nigeria. The main challenge is that the regulatory body, Nigeria Universities Commission (NUC) has not made it mandatory for higher institutions to include it into the curriculum. Other known challenges include long protocols and processes that must be followed during program approvals/accreditations by NUC at the universities, universities must follow the approved BMAS. New programs/departments, curriculum must be approved by NUC after which it must go through the university highest decision body (The senate) for final approval. Lack of enough experts in AI ethics field and having the right tools to work with. Not having access to AI ethics courses and, getting lecturers to include it in their lecture material since it is not in the approved curriculum. Lack of an AI code of ethics, and existing documents regulating AI ethics, may hinder the development of new applications for intelligent devices in the future (Słoniec and Kaczorowska 2020).

There are challenges of lack of well-equipped AI laboratories and hubs in the universities with the necessary technical tools for data collection.

6 Solution to Challenges of Integrating AI Ethics into Higher Education Curricula in West Africa

Figure 6 shows the process involved in accreditation of all programs in Nigeria universities. NUC accreditation for all higher institutions in Nigeria is done every five years. Programs undergo accreditation and can only function if they obtain full accreditation after following the protocols and rules laid down by NUC. Higher institutions must use the BMAS from NUC.

Nigeria universities being the case study in this work, already has AI BMAS in its curricula. To integrate AI ethics into Nigerian universities curriculum, potential efforts should be made by NUC (who happens to be the major stakeholder in Nigerian higher institutions), to make it mandatory for higher institutions to include AI ethics into the curriculum, for its complete integration and implementation which

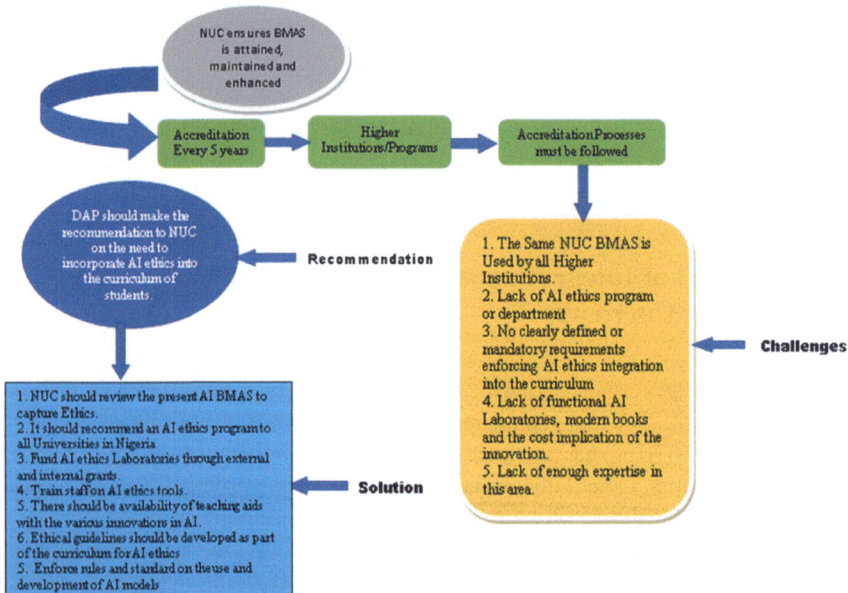

Fig. 6 NUC course integration/accreditation process

is expected to be practical driven. AI ethics awareness should be created at higher institutions focusing on technology, governance, and legal aspects. Stand-alone AI Ethics program/department should be made mandatory for all higher institutions.

Experts should be engaged who understand how to evaluate the impact of these systems on our society, particularly in terms of learning how to work effectively with AI systems and harness them for good. These experts should train the trainer on how to integrate ethics into AI curriculum and use AI ethics tools and stick to the existing ethics and standards of developing AI ethics systems.

Government should equip higher institutions with the necessary technical tools, AI laboratories, and modern books to expertly navigate AI ethical challenges. For good AI research, AI Hubs should be established.

Nigerian Universities and Africa Universities in general needs more of this Hubs from the government, private industry, professional organizations, and tech companies, to solve local problems in Nigeria and in Africa in general. Government should develop, and implement AI ethics standards and regulations, extend governance platforms by including AI stakeholders, academia, and practitioners in the governance bodies. They should develop and implement policies and guidelines that will help to build a strong data foundation that is fair and of good quality. There is a need to develop and implement ethical and regulatory frameworks along with sustainable mechanisms to unlock the availability and value of data to maximize the use of AI while limiting possible harms (Romanoff and Hidalgo-Sanchis 2019).

AI Ethics education should be made more accessible to everyone through E-learning. Integrating AI Ethics into the West African Universities' curricula will help to examine the most pressing ethical issues related to AI.

7 Conclusion

AI Ethics could potentially offer benefits to lecturers, researchers, and students in the form of personalized learning and pedagogical agents designed to deliver appropriate and sequenced content and feedback to learners. However, AI is still in a relatively early stage of development for education and there is much work to be done around the ethical and legal frameworks that can ensure that the technology is used for good and not harm, and that transparent processes are in place to ensure accountability at classroom, University community, and University systems levels. Academia's, University leaders and policymakers should be engaged with developments in AI ethics for education and the society, to empower students and researchers in the present and for future change.

References

Borenstein, J., and A. Howard. 2021. Emerging challenges in AI and the need for AI ethics education. *AI and Ethics* 1 (1): 61–65. https://doi.org/10.1007/s43681-020-00002-7.

Eleanor, B., F. Jasmin, R., Nicola, Jenner, R. Larbey, E., Weitkamp, and A. Winfield. 2020. The Ethics of Artificial Intelligence: Issues and Initiatives. *European Parliamentary Research Service*.

Furey, H., and F. Martin. 2018. AI Education Matters: A Modular Approach to AI Ethics Education. *AI Matters* 4 (4): 13–15. https://doi.org/10.1145/3299758.3299764.

Girard, E. 2020. *Digital Vision: Ethics*. 36. https://atos.net/wp-content/uploads/2020/04/atos-digital-vision-ethics-opinion-paper.pdf.

Gwagwa, A. 2019. Recommendations on the Inclusion Sub-Saharan Africa in Global AI Ethics. Research ICT Africa. RANITP Policy Brief 2. https://researchictafrica.net/wp/wp-content/uploads/2020/11/.

Hoes, F. 2019. *The Importance of Ethics in Artificial Intelligence*. https://towardsdatascience.com/the-importance-of-ethics-in-artificial-intelligence-16af073dedf8.

Hashmi, A. 2019. *AI Ethics: The Next Big Thing in Government*, 24.

O'Brien, J. 2020. *Digital Ethics in Higher Education: 2020*, 29. https://er.educause.edu/-/media/files/articles/2020/5/er20_2103.pdf.

Romanoff, M., and P. Hidalgo-Sanchis. 2019. *Building Ethical AI Approaches in the African Context UN Global Pulse*. https://www.unglobalpulse.org/2019/08/ethical-ai-approaches-in-the-african-context/.

Siau, K., and W. Wang. 2020. Artificial Intelligence (AI) Ethics: Ethics of AI and Ethical AI. *Journal of Database Management* 31 (2): 73–87. https://doi.org/10.4018/JDM.2020040105.

Słoniec, J., and A. Kaczorowska. 2020. *On in Artificial Intelligence*, 44–60. https://www.researchgate.net/publication/349311663.

Southgate, E., K., Blackmore, S., Pieschl, S., Grimes, J., McGuire, and K. Smithers. 2018. *Short Read: Artificial Intelligence and School Education*. University of Newcastle. https://creativecommons.org/licenses/by/4.0/.

Vincent, J. 2017. *Elon Musk Says We Need to Regulate AI Before it Becomes a Danger to Humanity—The Verge*. The Verge. https://www.theverge.com/2017/7/17/15980954/elon-musk-ai-regulation-existential-threat.

Open Access This chapter is licensed under the terms of the Creative Commons Attribution 4.0 International License (http://creativecommons.org/licenses/by/4.0/), which permits use, sharing, adaptation, distribution and reproduction in any medium or format, as long as you give appropriate credit to the original author(s) and the source, provide a link to the Creative Commons license and indicate if changes were made.

The images or other third party material in this chapter are included in the chapter's Creative Commons license, unless indicated otherwise in a credit line to the material. If material is not included in the chapter's Creative Commons license and your intended use is not permitted by statutory regulation or exceeds the permitted use, you will need to obtain permission directly from the copyright holder.

Promoting AI Ethics Through Awareness and Case Studies

Patrick E. McSharry

1 Introduction

Artificial intelligence (AI) is enabling organizations to address a range of real-world challenges in areas as diverse as global health, education and poverty alleviation. AI is flourishing at present because of advances in computer power, availability of large amounts of digital information (big data, open data), and enhanced theoretical understanding. John McCarthy coined the term Artificial Intelligence (AI) and described the field as the "science and engineering of making intelligent machines, especially intelligent computer programs" (McCarthy 1956). AI is based on the use of mathematical models to process large quantities of data and make accurate predictions. However, despite AI's contributions, we must remain constantly aware of the potential risks and shortcomings of AI, as well as instances where it may fail to be fit for purpose, in order to develop the best methods for teaching AI ethics.

Students of statistics learn that an influential pioneer of statistical modelling, George Box, famously stated that "All models are wrong, some are useful" (Box 1976). Box was concerned about two separate issues. First, model accuracy, understood through the principle of Occam's Razor, implies that the scientist should seek the simplest description of natural phenomena that is highly predictive. Second, Box was worried that scientists were not sufficiently aware when constructing models and explained "since all models are wrong the scientist must be alert to what is importantly wrong". Box realized that the model shortcomings were often due to the failure of the scientist to be sufficiently aware of the importance of the ingredients of the model. The potential pitfalls that await AI systems may be inferred from the comments of another famous statistician, David Cox, who explained "the idea that

---

P. E. McSharry (✉)
Regional ICT Center of Excellence, Carnegie Mellon University Africa, Kigali BP 6150, Rwanda

African Center of Excellence in Data Science, University of Rwanda, Kigali BP 4285, Rwanda

Oxford Man Institute of Quantitative Finance, Oxford University, Oxford OX2 6ED, UK

© The Author(s) 2023
C. C. Corrigan et al. (eds.), *AI Ethics in Higher Education: Insights from Africa and Beyond*, SpringerBriefs in Ethics, https://doi.org/10.1007/978-3-031-23035-6_6

complex physical, biological or sociological systems can be exactly described by a few formulae is patently absurd" (Cox 1995).

Awareness of the risks associated with AI can be improved by learning from case studies based on prior events and the consideration of future scenarios. Of course, there will always be new issues that arise and therefore AI practitioners will need to be kept up to date with the best practices. A greater danger may result from the potentially adverse impacts that certain AI applications could have on society at large. Without actively considering and analysing the long-term implications of AI on our everyday lives or making a conscious decision to accept these changes, citizens may be blindly walking into a new paradigm that is often referred to as the age of the Fourth Revolution.

Africa is home to over 1.3 billion people, and it is demographically the world's youngest continent with a median age of 19.7 years (UN 2019). The continent is already harnessing the potential of digital technology to revolutionize children's education with Ed-Tech solutions. An example of this is the $1 XPRIZE recipient, RoboTutor, an open-source Android tablet app from Carnegie Mellon University, that enables children aged seven to ten with little or no access to schools and teachers to learn basic reading, writing, and arithmetic without adult assistance (XPRIZE 2019). The AI-enabled RoboTutor addresses the acute shortage of teachers in developing countries and a Swahili version is now being tested in Tanzania. Whilst RoboTutor offers incredible opportunities for children who have access to this technology, consideration also needs to be given to the constraints that may prevent some children from accessing technology and the risks that this may have in terms of exacerbating inequalities and leaving some groups behind.

AI offers the ability to improve and speed up processes and scale applications. The many advantages of AI must be balanced with the potential for failure when implementing solutions in the real-world. Imperfect datasets, inadequate models and insufficient time to trial and test AI solutions may deliver a reputational blow to the entire field. Biased grading and scoring of individuals from minority groups and propagation of misinformation are just two of the risks that are already associated with AI. The time is ripe, therefore, to consider not only the important role of AI in delivering tailor-made education to create equal opportunities for all, but also the ethics of AI and how it will impact the lives of different groups within society. Politicians, business leaders and regulators face many challenging decisions as they embrace the immediate opportunities offered by AI and consider the long-term consequences for society. By priming educators and students in the field of AI with a heightened awareness of the risks, it is hoped that many adverse consequences can be mitigated and that AI can be used for the greater good.

This chapter aims to describe the advantages and disadvantages of AI using real-world examples, establish a set of risks to consider, and finally presents a set of scenarios that can help to stimulate discussion and debate before implementing such solutions. Many of the examples of the opportunities, challenges, risks and consequences discussed here are based on experiences at CMU-Africa, located in Rwanda, and case studies from the East Africa region. Participation in the development of Rwanda's National Strategy for AI has also been an enormous source of inspiration for this chapter, especially for devising scenarios to frame and explore the ethical risks. The following sections are structured to convey both the incredible opportunities offered by AI alongside the risks and ethical issues that AI presents. The first section introduces a series of examples from different African countries to demonstrate the benefits of AI and the advantages that are already being recognized. The second section considers the many facets of risk that come with the introduction of AI. While the main focus is on what we know at present, no guidance for the ethics of AI would be complete without discussing potential risks, future concerns and fears. Some guidelines are offered where possible to help identify and hopefully avoid problems with AI. These case studies serve to highlight the potential dangers that exist and how these are already shaping our world. It will be argued that the greatest risks to society are yet to come. By being aware and prepared for these risks, however, we will be better placed to mitigate against them.

2 Opportunities

Perhaps the most exciting proposition of the field of AI is the ability to facilitate innovation in so many aspects of our lives. The resulting changes are often dramatic and difficult for many to imagine without the help of science fiction novels. Virtual assistants, chatbots, digital communication and driverless cars are changing the way we interact and connect across the entire planet. This section outlines the diversity of ongoing initiatives across the continent and highlights a number of actual real-world use cases.

AI is at the heart of this global digital revolution, often referred to as the fourth industrial revolution. The first industrial revolution used water and steam power to mechanize production. The second used electric power to create mass production. The third used electronics and information technology to automate production. Schwab (2015) describes how a fourth industrial revolution is building on the third, the digital revolution that has been occurring since the middle of the last century. It is characterized by a fusion of technologies that is blurring the lines between the physical, digital, and biological spheres. The hallmark of the fourth industrial revolution is the automation of traditional manufacturing and industrial practices, using innovative smart technology.

The increasing availability of data from multiple sources, often referred to as big data, combined with advances in computational power and sophisticated mathematical algorithms is driving this innovation (Thomas and McSharry 2015). The internet of things (IoT) is changing the way we interact with the physical world and satellite imagery can help us to monitor the environment around us. Big data algorithms are able to harness information about our movements, online searches, financial transactions, comments and opinions in order to generate predictive analytics and improve decision-making. This treasure chest of knowledge about the demand for and supply of goods and services will lead to more efficient allocation of resources. The scalability offered by cloud computing is helping to speed up the pace of human development and will be a key component in achieving many of the sustainable development goals (SDGs).

In 2016, at the World Economic Forum (WEF) for Africa, it was acknowledged that Africa can use the fourth industrial revolution to enhance economic growth and prosperity. While technology has the potential to offer transformative power, it was also recognized that in order to maximise this opportunity, education on the continent is in need of radical reform. The Centre for the Fourth Industrial Revolution (C4IR) Rwanda, a partner of the WEF Network for Global Technology Governance, was founded with the objective of bringing together government, industry, civil society, and academia in order to co-design, test and refine policy frameworks and governance protocols to maximize the benefits and minimize the risks of 4IR technologies. C4IR Rwanda is primarily focusing on AI and data policy and developing multi-stakeholder partnerships to drive innovation and adoption at scale for the benefit of society.

Carnegie Mellon University Africa (CMU-Africa) launched a new Master of Science in Engineering Artificial Intelligence (MS EAI) in 2021 in recognition of the increasing demand from students that wish to integrate AI into their engineered solutions. The degree combines the fundamentals of AI and machine learning with engineering domain knowledge. The MS EAI takes AI and embeds it into engineering frameworks, including engineering representations, applications within engineered systems, and discipline-specific interpretations of system outcomes. Within these frameworks, students will learn to invent, tune, and specialize AI algorithms and tools for engineering systems. MS EAI graduates engineer new solutions where AI is integral to the engineered system's design or operation.

In its national strategy for AI, Rwanda plans to increase the number of individuals with experience in machine learning, data science, data engineering and computer science. In addition to these high-tech areas, there will also be a drive to develop practical technical skills in data collection, cleansing, processing and labelling. There will be a push to develop holistic curricula for science, technology, engineering and mathematics (STEM) subjects in order to prepare youth for these jobs in AI. Finally, there needs to be a business case for AI adoption. Attention will be given to human-centred design, identifying and piloting use cases and ensuring that there will be sufficient demand and uptake.

It is difficult to know where to start when listing the many AI innovations that are already under development across the African continent. The following examples in energy, finance and healthcare serve to highlight the wide range of interventions and applications using AI that are taking place in different countries across the continent.

There are many examples of AI-driven innovative pay-as-you-go financing models that allow customers to get instant access to products or services, while building ownership over time through flexible micro-payments. This innovation utilizes the widespread penetration of mobile phones in many countries. M-KOPA, based in Kenya, is an example of a connected asset financing platform that helps under-banked customers obtain access to products and services, such as electricity, radios, televisions and fridges.

Airtime in developing countries is quickly becoming a basic commodity among the rapidly growing middle class. Failure to have sufficient airtime in order to communicate or load data bundles is a challenge for many prepay customers. ComzAfrica, based in Rwanda, is a micro-lending company operating in 16 countries across Africa and Asia. ComzAfrica has built an Airtime Credit Service (ACS) which allows users to access airtime on a credit basis. Given that the users do not always have access to a retailer or direct funds, this service offered by both allows them to access airtime on a credit basis and make calls or send messages. Using actual loan data from ComzAfrica, it was shown that AI techniques could provide a credit scoring system that enables the company to quadruple the tolerable level of default rate for breaking even (Dushimimana et al. 2020).

Babylon Health is revolutionising healthcare by empowering doctors with AI in order to stand out from other providers. With operations in the US, UK and Canada, the company is known as Babyl in Rwanda. The speed provided by AI is a key differentiator as it helps medical professionals work faster, see more patients, and make better decisions based on user's data. Patients benefit by being able to address symptoms, get faster information about conditions, and proceed to treatment sooner. Its AI system learns from anonymised, aggregated, and consented medical datasets, patient health records, and the consultation notes from clinicians. Babylon is successfully showing how the power of AI can help address some of the healthcare challenges faced in countries with limited numbers of health professionals, enabling more speed and effectiveness in the processes that enable them to make decisions about triage, causes of symptoms, and future health predictions (Baker et al. 2020).

The anonymity afforded by digital technology and AI has also given rise to some unexpected innovations in healthcare. A study found that young people use Google to self-diagnose and treat when concerned about sexually transmitted diseases (PSI 2020). Sadly, it was fear that drives young people to turn to Google, rather than proactive measures to make healthy choices well before symptoms present. It was found that confidentiality is key and time efficiency is highly valued. Young people want sexual and reproductive health information at their fingertips, without others knowing what they are searching for. For these reasons, a chatbot designed and deployed in Kenya has been found to be much more accepted than a human adviser. Furthermore, a focus group highlighted how chatbots developed using "American" English failed to recognize slang commonly used by Kenyan youth. This frustrated users, resulting in decreased engagement. This important finding highlights the need for learning from local content and promoting home grown AI solutions that are more appropriate to the local context and needs of the local population.

3 Challenges and Risks

One of the biggest challenges for AI is how to ensure that it is inclusive, accessible and able to benefit those that are already digitally excluded. A large digital divide exists either due to digital illiteracy or through a lack of mobile connection (GSMA 2019).

AI requires data to work effectively, and unfortunately there is still an insufficient amount of accurate, complete and regularly updated data in many countries in Africa. The engine of an AI system relies on algorithms, which are sets of mathematical rules that process data. Without sufficient data from under-served communities, such as digital records and voice and text in multiple languages, there are risks that these algorithms, often trained on foreign data, will fail to be representative of African citizens and may be less accurate as a result. Furthermore, progress can only be truly made once data is being shared and available via application programming interface (APIs) that provide an interface for interactions between multiple software applications.

In the following sections, a number of potential risks are discussed. These are organised in terms of their severity and impact on society and categorized by three risks levels (Fig. 1). The three levels range from mainly unintended consequences of AI to purposeful intent to disrupt to extreme hazards with potential for substantial destruction. The first risk level is one that is already underway with countless examples having been encountered over the last decade. Fortunately, most of these risks can be mitigated to some extent by better awareness when designing AI systems and enhanced cybersecurity. In the case of the second risk level, there also exist extremely concerning examples involving criminal organizations that may have state sponsorship in some cases. Unfortunately, there are still few clear answers in terms of how to address and manage these risks. The good news is that considerable awareness of these risks now exist and numerous actors are attempting to find solutions. The third level of risk is futuristic for the moment but already of sufficient concern to warrant consideration and required immediate action in order to avoid potentially harmful consequences in the future.

In 2019, the European Commission, tasked with shaping Europe's digital future, produced a report entitled "Ethics guidelines for trustworthy AI" (EC 2019). According to this report, Trustworthy AI should be:

1. lawful—respecting all applicable laws and regulations;
2. ethical—respecting ethical principles and values; and
3. robust—both from a technical perspective while taking into account its social environment.

This summary of the report was presented to a class of students studying AI who were majoring in IT or electrical and computer engineering (ECE) at CMU-Africa

Fig. 1 List of escalating risks associated with AI and digitization

and CMU-Pittsburgh. The students were asked to identify, in their opinion, the most important component of trustworthy AI based on their own experiences. The 70 responses from students in the US and Africa were as follows: robust (47%), ethical (36%) and lawful (17%). This finding echoes the views of many engineering peers that ethics is something that others, perhaps sociologists or philosophers, should be concerned with, rather than AI practitioners. Engineers are already busy innovating and trying to make sure that the latest device, whether hardware, software or a combination, actually works. Given the technical specifications for a use case with clear demand, engineers often believe they are best left to solve problems rather than worrying about ethics.

Working in a silo and leaving the ethics for someone else to worry about might have been an acceptable solution if the pace of innovation were relatively slow and the new technology not so dangerous. It now appears, however, that AI is transforming rapidly with profound impacts and far-reaching implications for society, meaning that one cannot separate the creation and development of new interventions from the ethical discussions about their usage. For this reason, it is critical that the authorities regulating AI work closely with, and receive regular information from engineers in order to continuously review potential new risks as these arise.

The AI community is currently learning that applying models to socio-economic systems is fraught with danger and potential risks. While much progress has been made to avoid technical pitfalls such as overfitting and thereby ensuring parsimony and generalisability, there remain some serious issues with regard to data availability and quality that are more difficult to quantify. Many datasets are biased due to the way in which the data was collected or labelled. Concerning examples include sampling biases, crowd sourcing or alternative sources of big data that may not be representative of the population that is being addressed. These issues are particularly relevant for applications in African countries where due to limited research budgets, datasets are less likely to be available for building AI models. The use of some variables can prevent inclusion and discriminate against certain groups. Other variables serve as proxies to propagate existing biases. The importance of transparency and explainability is greater than ever in order for society to trust AI solutions.

The UK's Prime minister Boris Johnson discovered this the hard way. In August 2020, as a result of the COVID-19 pandemic and resulting lockdown restrictions which prevented children from attending schools and sitting exams, the UK's examination regulator Ofqual was obliged to develop a computer algorithm that could replace the need for examinations in order to grade all its A-level students (BBC 2020). As a result, approximately 39% of predicted A-level results were downgraded by the algorithm. Most shockingly, disadvantaged students were the most adversely affected as the algorithm replicated existing societal inequalities. Initially, Johnson claimed the grading algorithm was dependable and robust. As student protests increased, however, Johnson changed his position, claiming that it was AI which was responsible for the error and shedding the blame on what he called the 'mutant algorithm' for the exams fiasco, leading Ofqual to eventually override the algorithm (Guardian 2020). Though perhaps the first national large-scale disaster for an algorithm, it is certainly unlikely to be the last.

The less attractive consequence of the innovation promised by the fourth industrial revolution is the potential loss of many jobs as AI and automation replaces the less skilled workers within the labour force. Worse still, there is growing concern about the long-term societal impacts of AI, particularly as automation replaces many professional jobs and larger numbers of people find themselves unemployed. A seminal study estimated that about 47% of total US employment is at risk from automation (Frey and Osborne 2017). As the benefits of AI in business become more apparent and engineers enhance the applicability of AI, it is now clear that the machines are only getting warmed up. A closer look at the jobs that might be automated painted an even scarier picture, indicating that not only low-skilled repetitive jobs that are already affected by automation are in danger, but also a whole new set of higher skilled professional jobs, including lawyers and medical professionals (Brandes and Wattenhofer 2016). Given the low levels of human capital and scarcity of high-skilled jobs in the African continent, the future threat of automation is even greater.

Globalization is another major factor, often with an insatiable appetite for cheap labour by any means possible. Those developing countries that currently sell the cheap labour of their unskilled workers will face competition from AI on a global scale (Harari 2018). According to the World Economic Forum, AI is expected to replace 85 million jobs worldwide by 2025 (WEF 2020). The good news is that this report goes on to say that AI will also create 97 million new jobs in that same timeframe. The big question for teenagers in African countries when considering a career, is whether future opportunities may be threatened by an AI-enabled algorithm or machine that can eventually automate the tasks required in this sector. New technology such as AI chat-bots and the proliferation of 3D printers is likely to replace many unskilled workers that currently find employment in sweatshops and call centres. The bridge from cheap labour to high-skill tech jobs requires substantial investment in human capital development, and in particular in third level education with a focus on university degrees that offer AI skills such as data science, machine learning and cybersecurity. For this reason, Rwanda's national strategy for AI recommends a particular focus in these areas and also training for technical experts to collect, process and label datasets.

Road safety is one area where the automation of driving enabled by AI may both enhance safety while also replacing paid employment. Walking through the current issues and considering the future risks shows just how difficult it is for policymakers to safely manage the pace of AI innovation. Road injuries are now the biggest killer of children and young adults worldwide causing 1.35 million deaths each year which is more than that from HIV/Aids, tuberculosis or diarrhoeal diseases (WHO 2018). In addition, between 20 and 50 million people are seriously injured in road accidents each year (WB 2017). At present, 93% of the world's fatalities on the roads occur in low- and middle-income countries, even though these countries have only 60% of the world's vehicles. The cause of traffic accidents can be inferred from the US's fatality analysis reporting system (FARS). Road traffic deaths are almost entirely caused by human drivers due to alcohol abuse (29%), speeding (26%) or being distracted (21%) while driving (NHTSA 2019). Analysis of on-scene post-crash data concluded that the vast majority (93%) of critical reasons leading to crashes are attributable to the driver (Singh 2018). Self-driving cars, also known as autonomous vehicles, will make drivers redundant. By meticulously following traffic rules and communicating directly with other vehicles, they can improve road safety by never succumbing to the temptation to speed, drink, fall asleep or become distracted by telephone calls. There are of course serious risks to having a large fleet of autonomous vehicles and system failure or a cyberattack could lead to large-scale disaster.

While engineers are fast at innovating and creating new solutions, they are much slower to acknowledge or consider the potential misuses or nefarious implications of their inventions. The proliferation of the internet, mobile technology and countless social media platforms dominate our lives, and we have all been lured into the use of these platforms without actively given our consent or giving adequate consideration to the risks. The historian, Yuval Noah Harari, dedicates a lesson for the 21st Century to the dangers of AI and warns that society is currently facing unprecedented challenges from infotech and biotech (Harari 2018). While humans were forced to revolt against exploitation or retrain to overcome the first three industrial resolutions, Harari fears that many simply do not have the skills required to make the transition to working in high tech jobs. Automation is therefore likely to offer a worse outcome to many: irrelevance rather than exploitation.

The COVID-19 pandemic also demonstrated just how dispensable many jobs have become as many people lost their means of employment as some businesses have been forced to shut down, while other parts of the economy that rely on AI have gone from strength to strength. According to the ILO, 114 million jobs were lost globally in 2020 due to the pandemic (ILO 2020). In fact, this may be an underestimate, given that 8.8% of global working hours were lost for the whole of last year (relative to the fourth quarter of 2019), equivalent to 255 million full-time jobs. Roughly 9.6 million U.S. workers (ages 16–64) lost their jobs. In contrast, only about 2.6 million workers in the EU lost their jobs over this period. This is remarkable given that the EU is home to about 100 million more people than the U.S. The two geographical areas contribute equally to the world economy, each accounting for about 16% of global output. The reason for this is that countries across the EU deployed significant employment retention schemes, while the U.S. focused on stimulus checks and unemployment compensation in lieu of job retention. These different policies may have profound implications in the future, especially when the opportunity to replace workers with AI become more of a reality. While the industrial revolution created the working class, AI may be already creating a "global useless class", a term coined by Yuval Harari to emphasize the level of exclusion that could be caused by automation (Harari 2018). The response to COVID-19 has clarified how governments will likely respond to further automation.

AI and automation have played a large role in helping many big tech companies to reap the rewards from scaling up their operations and services. Apple became the world's first trillion-dollar company in August 2018. Two years later, right in the middle of the pandemic, Apple crossed the two trillion-dollar hurdle. A handful of big tech companies, known as the FANGAM stocks, Facebook, Amazon, Netflix, Google owner Alphabet, Apple and Microsoft, are key players in AI and have all increased in value steadily over the last decade. In 2020, Apple, Microsoft, Amazon,

Google and Facebook had a 21.7% share of the S&P500—an index representing 500 of the largest companies listed on stock exchanges in the US. Investors that use fundamentals to value companies claim that the stock market has become detached from economic reality. Forward-looking AI enthusiasts argue that that these tech companies represent our new reality as they process most of our interactions with digital technology, while others are terrified by the huge control and power these companies now hold over many of us.

The response to an extreme event is a good way to test the resilience of any business model. The global pandemic, COVID-19, that has claimed more than 3.5 million lives as of Jun-2021, produced such an event. The impact on different parts of the economy help to understand which companies are likely to survive going forward and AI certainly features strongly. During 2020, global lockdowns caused the S&P500 index to crash by 34% in March but it ended the year up more than 18%. Two-thirds of that gain was entirely due to the growth of the six FANGAM stocks, which registered average growth of over forty percent during the year. The resilience of big tech is apparent by the fact that these companies continued to make money despite the majority of the global population being locked down and unable to leave their homes. It is the use of information technology and AI that allows these big tech companies to scale and grow at unprecedented rates. The effect of COVID-19, with many traditional workers furloughed and paid to stay at home without working, has served to demonstrate that the concept of the global useless class may no longer be futuristic.

3.1 Risk Level 2

There are already some noticeable risks that are being facilitated by social media and exacerbated by AI. One such risk is the proliferation of fake news described as false or misleading information presented as news. A more sinister view is that this fake news is specially crafted disinformation with the sole aim of damaging the reputation of a person, company or nation. There are increasing concerns that fake news can influence political, economic, and social well-being. Indeed, fake news is frequently mentioned as having had an impact on many political elections, such as the 2016 UK Brexit referendum and the 2016 US presidential election with Trump versus Clinton.

Fake news spreads much more rapidly on social networks such as Twitter than real news because people are more likely to share extreme and unlikely news than the mundane (Vosoughi et al. 2018). Falsehood diffused significantly farther, faster, deeper, and more broadly than the truth in all categories of information, and the effects were more pronounced for false political news than for false news about terrorism, natural disasters, science, urban legends, or financial information. Along with the long-term implications of large swathes of society being misinformed, some of the dire dangers of fake news are now acknowledged. The World Health Organization (WHO) coined the term "infodemic" to describe the misinformation surrounding

COVID-19 and how this has spread as fast as the virus itself. Sadly, conspiracy theories, rumours and cultural stigma have all contributed to deaths and injuries with a recent study estimating that about 5,800 people were admitted to hospital globally as a result of following false information received on social media (Islam et al. 2020).

There have been numerous cybersecurity incidents, involving espionage, fraud and ransomware, with a worrying upward trend in the past year. A recent study found that 86% of breaches were financially motivated, and 10% were motivated by espionage (Verizon 2020). Furthermore, 70% of breaches were perpetrated by external actors, and organized criminal groups were behind 55% of breaches. In May 2021, the infamous cyber-criminal entity, DarkSide, took offline a major US pipeline carrying 45% of the East Coast's supply of fuel, using a ransomware cyber-attack. As a result, the U.S. Department of Justice is elevating investigations of ransomware attacks to a similar priority as terrorism. While digitization and AI offers many opportunities, they also generate systemic vulnerabilities as a result of the digital connectivity required. Accenture, a global consulting firm, found that the number of business leaders spending more than 20% of IT budgets on advanced technology investments has doubled in the last three years and 69% of business leaders say that staying ahead of attackers is a constant battle and the cost is unsustainable (Accenture 2020).

3.2 Risk Level 3

Science fiction movies, like Terminator, make for thrilling entertainment by suggesting that AI may eventually destroy the human race. Unmanned aerial vehicles (UAVs), more commonly known as drones, are now routinely used for military missions by countries such as the US, China, Russia and Israel. It is generally assumed that humans are fully in control of the movements and actions of these drones. A United Nations report this year, however, suggests that a drone, used against militia fighters in Libya's civil war, may have selected a target autonomously (UNSC 2021). This drone, described as "a lethal autonomous weapons system," was powered by AI and used by government-backed forces against enemy militia fighters as they ran away from rocket attacks. The fighters "were hunted down and remotely engaged by the unmanned combat aerial vehicles or the lethal autonomous weapons systems," according to the report, which did not say whether there were any casualties or injuries. The weapons systems, it said, "were programmed to attack targets without requiring data connectivity between the operator and the munition: in effect a true 'fire, forget and find' capability." Rather than being a futuristic concern, this now demonstrates that the world has already embarked on a journey that will see the proliferation of AI-enabled military equipment.

Concerns about humans not being able to compete with robots or AI applications became mainstream in the 2010s. AI has already conquered chess, once viewed as the ultimate strategic game for humans—requiring superior intelligence and years of dedicated training. IBM's Deep Blue won its first game against the reigning world champion Garry Kasparov in 1996. Two decades later, AI systems can be trained solely via "self-play" and no longer need any human interaction or training. In 2017, Google's DeepMind team created AlphaZero, which within 24 h of training achieved a superhuman level of play in chess, shogi and go. With AI systems now capable of superhuman intelligence without the need for human inputs, it is fair to ask if a sophisticated AI system might one day decide that humans are no longer necessary.

An existential risk is an event that could lead to human extinction or permanently and drastically curtail humanity's potential. In contrast to global catastrophic risks, existential risk scenarios do not allow for meaningful recovery and are, by definition, unprecedented in human history. The likelihood of the world experiencing an existential catastrophe over the next one hundred years has been estimated to be high as a one in six risk (Ord 2020). A recent report identified the misuse of AI systems as a key extreme risk and calls on governments to prepare appropriately (Ord et al. 2021). The report explains that as AI becomes integrated into safety-critical systems, whether self-driving cars, air traffic control systems, or military equipment, it raises the stakes of accidents, malicious use of this technology, or AI systems behaving in unexpected ways and recommends increasing funding for technical AI safety research, to help avoid the dangers of unsafe AI systems.

These sections have walked through a series of risks and offered a three-level classification system based on the severity of the risk. At present, society appears to be moving consistently along this risk stratification. This is not surprising since greater adoption of AI brings with it the potential for more harmful consequences in both magnitude and spatial scale. Many of the level one risks are manageable and in isolation do not necessarily warrant the regulation of AI but certainly make a case for the ethics of AI. The level two risks are already taking being observed and some of the consequences may be difficult to reverse. Finally, level three risks are not science fiction and deserve serious consideration. Awareness of all these risks and better classification may help policymakers to manage the opportunities and threats of AI.

4 Risk Mitigation

Fortunately, there has been a dramatic awakening to the risks of AI over the last three years. Numerous organizations have attempted to introduce ethical principles and offer recommendations that will guide future practitioners and protect society. These include national governments (UK 2018), the European Union (EC 2019), intergovernmental economic organisations (OECD 2019), international consultations involving experts from 155 countries (UNESCO 2019), the world's largest technical professional organization (IEEE 2019) and one of the largest tech companies (Microsoft 2020).

The Government of Rwanda (GoR) represented by Rwanda's Ministry of ICT and Innovation (MINICT) and Rwanda Utilities Regulatory Authority (RURA) are collaborating with GIZ and the Future Society in a project called "FAIR Forward— Artificial Intelligence for all". Being part of the Future Society team collaborating

Promoting AI Ethics Through Awareness and Case Studies 79

with GoR and GIZ has provided many insights into the process for establishing national guidelines. It has been paramount to organize workshops, solicit expert feedback, and validate the AI ethical guidelines which are now being presented in Rwanda's National Artificial Intelligence Policy. CMU-Africa, which is based in Rwanda, will provide masters courses in IT and AI and undertake pilot studies that aim to ensure the following important AI guidelines are respected:

1. Societal Benefit: aim to deliver strong economic and social impact and improve the well-being of citizens
2. Inclusion & Fairness: identify underrepresentation in data and lack of access to services due to economic means, physical location or gender
3. Privacy: anonymize personal data and follow national privacy laws
4. Safety & Security: ensure data storage and sharing mechanisms are secure and encrypted
5. Responsibility & Accountability: consider and acknowledge the impact of AI for all participants and stakeholders
6. Transparency and Explainability: document all steps involved in the construction and deployment of an AI system
7. Human Autonomy and Dignity: maintain freedom from subordination to, or coercion by, AI systems.

With these guidelines in mind, the alertness of future AI experts to these issues is paramount. CMU-Africa promotes trustworthy AI solutions which are lawful, ethical and robust. With a new MSc in Engineering AI being offered by CMU, it is important to ensure that learners are fully aware of these principles of AI ethics. After presenting case studies in different sectors that highlight the opportunities and risks, it is useful to illustrate the potential danger of insufficient awareness and to study the dangers of privacy risks, lack of transparency and biases in data.

One way that has been tested and proven both useful and practical in classes at CMU-Africa and during policy workshops for the national AI strategy, is to initiate a group discussion about the risks and consequences of AI for a particular solution. This can be achieved by offering situation appropriate scenarios about how AI would be utilized in a given sector and how it might affect certain individuals. By focusing on scenarios that highlight situations where individuals experience the advantages and disadvantages of AI systems, it is then easier to assess what is fair and what might lead to exclusion or job losses for example. These scenarios need to be realistic, provide reasonable advantages as to be attractive and yet carefully highlight some of the potential pitfalls and adverse consequences. The discussions that follow in a group environment can then be focused around the seven guidelines listed above.

In order to maintain a thread running through the different scenarios and emphasize relevant issues to tackle, each scenario can be discussed in the light of some talking points. Breakout rooms offer a means of exploring multiple sectors in a small group setting and then bringing participants back to identify common themes. The following set of guiding questions can help to draw out important ethical issues for group discussion:

- What are the benefits of this AI system?
- Who will specifically benefit from the adoption of this AI system?
- Might the introduction of this AI system threaten existing jobs?
- Will certain individuals be adversely affected immediately or in the long term?
- Could accessing data for the AI system be a breach of privacy law?
- Might the changes introduced by this innovation lead to greater surveillance?
- Where and how should the data required for the AI system be stored?
- Will data be encrypted and who will have access?
- Are regulators or policymakers providing oversight of this innovation and its impact?
- Is it relatively easy to understand how the AI system operates?
- Does the introduction of this AI system remove the full and effective self determination of any individual over themselves?

In the boxes below, three scenarios are presented for banking, healthcare and education. Depending on the audience and context, these scenarios can be adapted and extended to include other sectors where AI is likely to play an important role.

> **Banking Scenario**
>
> Sandra is a student at the University studying data science with excellent grades. She works as a waiter at a restaurant at weekends. Due to the COVID-19 lockdown, her earnings have been reduced and she is concerned about running out of money.
>
> Just as Sandra is considering seeking a loan, she receives an SMS on her mobile phone from her bank offering a loan facility. She is amazed to find this pre-approved loan is exactly what she is looking for. She clicks on the link, accepts the loan through an app and finds the money in her bank account an hour later.
>
> Her bank has developed a credit scoring model that utilizes AI. Harnessing data about account activity, degree course and grades enables the bank to automatically select students for pre-approved loans. The speed and efficiency of processing these loans has increased the bank's profits and improved customer satisfaction.
>
> Sandra's friend John has been waiting for over a month to hear back from his bank about a paper-based loan application that took hours to complete. On hearing about Sandra's positive experience, John decides to switch banks.

Healthcare Scenario

Peter is married to Catherine and they have two children and live and work on the land in a thriving rural community, situated over 100 km from the capital city. One year ago, Peter subscribed to a new medical app on his phone that was offered as a reward for being a loyal customer with his mobile network operator (MNO). The app provides useful advice on nutrition and lifestyle and has been particularly useful for receiving information on COVID-19. Peter and Catherine were very fortunate in being able to attend good local schools and their high literacy levels have allowed them to learn from the medical app and make informed decisions that have benefited their family.

Recently Peter was pleasantly surprised to be offered medical insurance for a very reasonable monthly premium. He assumes that the enrollment information and data he was providing via the app over the year makes him an attractive client for the insurer that is collaborating with the MNO. Peter is delighted that he can now have peace of mind by knowing that his family are covered by medical insurance.

Peter's neighbour, Charles, is also a subscriber to the same MNO. He too is a farmer but due to past health problems has been unable to spend as much time on his land or to generate a regular income. As Charles cannot afford the money to make as many mobile phone calls, as Peter has, he has not been offered the medical app or the medical insurance.

Education Scenario

Marie is at the national university in the capital city where she studies medicine. Her family live in a smaller town, approximately three hours away. During the restrictions caused by the pandemic, Marie was relieved to find that the university was able to provide continuous education and was not forced to shut down. Fortunately, the forward-thinking administration in the university had invested substantially in IT equipment and fast broadband and were already experimenting with remote teaching for adjunct faculty living in other countries. As a result, the university was able to quickly move from physical classes to remote classes using Zoom, allowing students to continue their courses even when in a different part of the country. A partnership with an Ed-Tech company helped to streamline the process and offer additional courses and online materials.

Marie enjoys the security of being at home with her parents and siblings during the lockdowns and can still continue with her dream of becoming the first doctor in her family. Lecturers at the University have welcomed the advantages of the Ed-Tech platform, which includes tailored digital content, AI-enabled chat-bots and communication channels for students working on group projects.

> Marie's older brother, George, is in his final year at a different university. The board of this university decided not to invest in IT and are relatively inflexible with regard to new technology, insisting that all lectures take place physically on campus. Sadly, this university now has no choice but to postpone all activities until the following year.

5 Conclusions

Although John McCarthy coined the term AI in 1955, many of the original hopes for this new technology have only recently been realized. From being able to beat humans at chess, shogi and go to empowering autonomous vehicles to promoting human development, AI will continue to enable innovations that were previously unimaginable. Alongside the considerable opportunities offered by AI, politicians and leaders need to be wary of the risks posed by AI. These risks have the potential not only to adversely affect individuals but could possibly threaten democracy and have a profound negative impact on society. By being aware of these risks and constantly discussing the scenarios that will likely play out over time, it may be possible to mitigate against the worst of these risks and harness the opportunities that AI can offer.

References

Accenture. 2020. Third Annual State of Cyber Resilience. Accenture, USA. https://www.accenture.com/_acnmedia/PDF-116/Accenture-Cybersecurity-Report-2020.pdf.

Baker, A., Y. Perov, K., Middleton, J., Baxter, D., Mullarkey, D., Sangar, M., Butt, and A. DoRosario. 2020. A Comparison of Artificial Intelligence and Human Doctors for the Purpose of Triage and Diagnosis. *Frontiers in Artificial Intelligence Medicine and Public Health*. https://doi.org/10.3389/frai.2020.543405.

BBC. 2020. A-Levels: Algorithm at Centre of Grading Crisis 'Unlawful'. BBC.

Box, G.E.P. 1976. Science and Statistics (PDF). *Journal of the American Statistical Association* 71 (356): 791–799.

Brandes, P., and R. Wattenhofer. 2016. Opening the Frey/Osborne Black Box: Which Tasks of a Job are Susceptible to Computerization? arXiv:1604.08823.

Cox, D.R. 1995. Comment on "Model uncertainty, data mining and statistical inference." *Journal of the Royal Statistical Society, Series A* 158: 455–456.

Dushimimana, B., Y. Wambui, T. Lubega, and P.E. McSharry. 2020. Use of Machine Learning Techniques to Create a Credit Score Model for Airtime Loans. *Journal of Risk and Financial Management* 13 (8): 180.

EC. 2019. Ethics Guidelines for Trustworthy AI. European Commission, Brussels, Belgium. https://ec.europa.eu/digital-single-market/en/news/ethics-guidelines-trustworthy-ai.

Frey, C.B., and M.A. Osborne. 2017. The Future of Employment: How Susceptible are Jobs to Computerisation? *Technological Forecasting & Social Change* 114 (2017): 254–280.
Guardian. 2020. Boris Johnson Blames 'Mutant Algorithm' for Exams Fiasco. https://www.theguardian.com/politics/2020/aug/26/boris-johnson-blames-mutant-algorithm-for-exams-fiasco.
GSMA. 2019. Connected Society—Closing the Coverage Gap: How Innovation Can Drive Rural Connectivity. https://www.gsma.com/mobilefordevelopment/wp-content/uploads/2019/07/GSMA-Closing-The-Coverage-Gap-How-Innovation-Can-Drive-Rural-Connectivity-Report-2019.pdf.
Harari, Y.N. 2018. *21 Lessons for the 21st Century*. London, UK: Jonathan Cape.
IEEE. 2019. The IEEE Global Initiative on Ethics of Autonomous and Intelligent Systems. Ethically Aligned Design: A Vision for Prioritizing Human Well-being with Autonomous and Intelligent Systems, Institute of Electrical and Electronics Engineers (IEEE). https://ethicsinaction.ieee.org.
ILO. 2020. ILO Monitor: COVID-19 and the World of Work, Seventh edn.
Islam, M.S., T. Sarkar, S.H. Khan, A.-H.M. Kamal, S.M.M. Hasan, A. Kabir, D. Yeasmin, M.A. Islam, K.I.A. Chowdry, K.S. Anwar, A.A. Chughtai, and H. Seale. 2020. COVID-19–Related Infodemic and Its Impact on Public Health: A Global Social Media Analysis. *The American Journal of Tropical Medicine and Hygiene* 103 (4): 1621–1629.
McCarthy, J. 1956. Dartmouth Summer Research Project on Artificial Intelligence. Dartmouth College, Hanover, New Hampshire, US.
Microsoft. 2020. Responsible AI Principles, Microsoft, Seattle, US. https://www.microsoft.com/en-us/ai/responsible-ai.
NHTSA. 2019. Annual 2019 traffic fatality data from the Fatality Analysis Reporting System (FARS). National Highway Traffic Safety Administration, U.S. Department of Transportation, US.
OECD. 2019. Principles on AI, Paris, France. http://www.oecd.org/going-digital/ai/principles/.
Ord, T. 2020. *The Precipice: Existential Risk and the Future of Humanity*. London, UK: Bloomsbury Publishing.
Ord, T., A. Mercer, and S. Dannreuther. 2021. *Future Proof: The Opportunity to Transform the UK's Resilience to Extreme Risks*. The Centre for long term resilience: Oxford University, Oxford, UK.
PSI. 2020. *Adolescents & Youth, Digital Health Solutions, Sexual and Reproductive Health*. Nairobi, Kenya: Population Services International.
Schwab, K. 2015. *The Fourth Industrial Revolution: What It Means and How to Respond*. Foreign Affairs.
Singh, S. 2018. *Critical Reasons for Crashes Investigated in the National Motor Vehicle Crash Causation Survey*. Traffic Safety Facts Crash Stats. Report No. DOT HS 812 506). Washington, DC: National Highway Traffic Safety Administration.
Thomas, R., and P.E. McSharry. 2015. *Big Data Revolution*. London: Wiley.
UNESCO. 2019. Normative Instrument on AI Ethics, Paris, France. https://en.unesco.org/artificial-intelligence/ethics.
UN. 2019. World Population Prospects 2019, Online Edition. Rev. 1". United Nations, Department of Economic and Social Affairs, Population Division.
UNSC. 2021. Letter dated 8 March 2021 from the Panel of Experts on Libya established pursuant to resolution 1973 (2011) addressed to the President of the Security Council S/2021/229, United Nations Security Council, Geneva, Switzerland.
UK. 2018. AI Code of Ethics. UK House of Lords. https://publications.parliament.uk/pa/ld201719/ldselect/ldai/100/100.pdf.
Verizon. 2020. Data Breach Investigations Report. Verizon, USA. https://enterprise.verizon.com/resources/reports/2020-data-breach-investigations-report.pdf.
Vosoughi, S., D. Roy, and S. Aral. 2018. The Spread of True and False News Online. *Science* 359 (6380): 1146–1151. https://doi.org/10.1126/science.aap9559.
WHO. 2018. Global Status Report on Road Safety. World Health Organization.
WB. 2017. The High toll of Traffic Injuries: Unacceptable and Preventable. World Bank.
WEF. 2020. The Future of Jobs Report 2020. Geneva, Switzerland: World Economic Forum.

XPRIZE. 2019. Global Learning XPRIZE. https://www.xprize.org/prizes/global-learning.

Open Access This chapter is licensed under the terms of the Creative Commons Attribution 4.0 International License (http://creativecommons.org/licenses/by/4.0/), which permits use, sharing, adaptation, distribution and reproduction in any medium or format, as long as you give appropriate credit to the original author(s) and the source, provide a link to the Creative Commons license and indicate if changes were made.

The images or other third party material in this chapter are included in the chapter's Creative Commons license, unless indicated otherwise in a credit line to the material. If material is not included in the chapter's Creative Commons license and your intended use is not permitted by statutory regulation or exceeds the permitted use, you will need to obtain permission directly from the copyright holder.

The Future: Visions for Responsible AI Developers

AI Ethics Education for Future African Leaders

Gadosey Pius Kwao, Deborah Dormah Kanubala, and Belona Sonna

1 Ethics in the African Context

From the Greek word "ethos", which means custom, habit or character, the word ethics can mean and has been defined in many different ways by ethics and morality theorists. Some define ethics as a branch of moral philosophy concerned with asking questions about what is right or wrong. Others might say they are a set of guiding principles for an individual or group. In these modern times, it is advisable to desist from being in a hurry to pick up an individual or group's view of what may be termed as ethical or unethical. Therefore, we can say that the way ethics is understood is heavily influenced by one's geographical and cultural differences.

Across the world and especially in Africa, a person's ethical decisions cannot be separated from their beliefs and societal expectations. In order to define ethics in the African context, however, caution must be taken so that a "one size fits all approach" is not adopted with the assumption that situations are the same everywhere. All the same, it is safe to assume that the fundamentals of "African Ethics" stems from the importance of the interactions between individuals and their communities and what they perceive to be morally "good" or "bad" and "right" or "wrong".

It is also nearly impossible to consider ethics in the African context without considering religion as a relevant contributing factor to how it is defined. Religion has always played a big role in society's determination of what is considered morally wrong or right but their fundamental beliefs, regardless of the type of religion, are almost the same. With the limits of AI capabilities being pushed, many questions that religious communities will ask will be related to how far A.I should be allowed to go.

G. P. Kwao
Computer Science Department, Lancaster University, Bailrigg, Ghana

D. D. Kanubala (✉)
Saarbrücken Graduate School of Computer Science, Saarbrucken, Germany

B. Sonna
Australian National University and BEL'S AI Initiative, Canberra, Australia

If any technology could make autonomous decisions just like any person, must it also be considered a person? Are we then challenging the belief that humans are the only beings on earth with a purpose for God? The theological term "Imago Dei" which is Latin for "Image of God" refers to the relationship between humans and their creator. Is creating in our own image and trusting that creation other than God the creator not a practice of idolatry? (Herzfeld 2002). Aside that all religions believe there is a creator and for instance some believe in Jesus Christ and others in Mohammed, but whichever their belief is they hold true that there is one supreme one and none can be compared to their creator. They believe it is only their Supreme being that has the power to create intelligence that can think and act like a human. The bigger question here; Is it ethical to encourage the building of "human-like" machines?

One may first need to ask: how is defining ethics relevant in teaching AI in Africa? AI or any other digital technology is logically malleable and exhibits a high level of flexibility. Its intentions are therefore very open to any kind of interpretation. This means that AI can be used for countless purposes, which may or may not be aligned with the objectives of its developers (Stahl 2021).

One factor that influences use and objectives is culture, which of course varies widely by geographical location. Culture is dynamic and one major contributor to change in cultural beliefs and practices today has been the influx of Information Technology over the past few decades. However, just like any other phenomenon, embracing AI in any culture means that people may have to stop doing and seeing in the ways they were accustomed to. However, people are naturally hesitant towards immediate change. Therefore, successful implementation of this change (the use of AI) starts happening when people start seeing the need for it and believe that it will improve their lives, while not violating their cultural values.

In short, "African Ethics" in AI may be defined as the set of guiding principles and methodologies applied in the building and usage of AI in Africa that are widely accepted by communities majorly based on their beliefs and what stakeholders believe as being morally right and do not infringe on fundamental human rights, while improving lives.

1.1 Ethical Principles

AI ethics is a set of features and techniques used during the lifecycle of AI projects in order to ensure that the final solutions protect the end users from potential harm such as bias and discrimination, denial of individual autonomy, unfair outcomes, invasion of privacy. Thus, AI ethics is led by some principles that bring ethical values to AI systems. Principles here can be defined as a set of concepts and rules for the use and development of AI. Values are not mere desire, but goals and ideals that people endorse thoughtfully and defend as appropriate or right (Leslie 2019). In this section, the most common principles of AI recognised by many communities will be discussed as well as the values that are related to them. Then, some tensions that may exist between values will be highlighted.

Overall, AI Ethics principles are meant to ensure trustworthy AI. Many concepts have been proposed by different communities or institutions as the key requirements for AI ethics. Recently, in April 2021, we witnessed the proposal of AI regulation by the European Union Commission that is based on seven core pillars including human agency oversight, technical robustness and safety, privacy and data protection, transparency, diversity—non-discrimination and fairness, social environmental wellbeing and accountability. The government of Australia published another set of concepts of ethical AI that are made up of accountability, transparency, reliability, privacy protection, fairness, human-center values and finally social and environmental wellbeing (Department of Industry 2019). Lo Piano (2020) reviewed many other propositions coming from other institutions and came out with a set of principles that were common to them including transparency, justice and fairness, non-maleficence and privacy. Be it as it is, the most important principles of ethics are listed as follows: respect of human rights, respect of society and environment, robustness and safety, transparency, contestability, responsibility, justice and fairness, and privacy. (AIHLEG 2019). In this section, we would review each of these principles.

Respect of Human rights refers to all the values that preserves human autonomy. The two key values of this principle are human dignity and equality. In the context of AI, the system should not compel people to make decisions that they can't assume as human rights and are inalienable. In addition, the system should treat people equally without any discrimination regarding the nationality, gender, and place of living, as human rights are universal. Finally, the system should not ignore any one of the human rights as they are indivisible, interdependent and interrelated.

Respect for society and the environment is all about making AI systems serve people by respecting the rules of society and the environment where the system will be used. The values aligned with this principle are sustainability, environmental friendliness, and social impact.

Robustness and safety is related to all aspects of the system that make it reliable in accordance with the intended purpose. The values assigned to this principle are accuracy, security, resilience to attack, and reproducibility.

Transparency principle focuses on the break of the traditional black box process. There should be clarity and understanding on the output of the system as well as traceability of the process used. This characteristic brings values such as explainability, interaction, and communication that are important to improve the truth of the final users with respect to the system.

Responsibility or Accountability aims to point out who is responsible for the outcomes of the system. One of the reasons for the less adoption of AI based solutions is that there is no organization or individual that can endorse the system in case of harm. For example, should the designer of the AI solution or the owner who employs it or the society that uses it be the one to accept a faulty model? For now, it is not clear. However, research is ongoing to figure out a solution that suits everyone. Thus the most significant value linked to the principle is auditability and values related to the transparency principle.

Justice and fairness ensure that AI systems are equitable, inclusive and fair with respect to all the potential users of the solution. The values related to this principle are non-discrimination, accessibility, universal design and stakeholder participation.

Privacy claims the respect of privacy rights and data protection in an AI system. Basically, throughout the lifecycle of the system, privacy should be preserved by using appropriate techniques. Techniques such as data anonymisation and differential privacy could be used to preserve dataset for hacking. This principle brings along values such as security, quality and integrity of data, access to data (Ethical and Societal Implications of Data and Arti 2019).

In general, the values are tangible means used to assess if an AI ethics principle is respected or not. Hence, when designing a particular system for a specific purpose, it is necessary to bring people from different backgrounds to propose a set of values that can be used to assess AI ethics principle without any restriction. The values listed above are not exhaustive and can be contextualised during the application in the real world. For instance in healthcare, there are values such as quality of service, aggressiveness of a treatment that can be used to assess the quality of an AI system.

However, for the same system, there can be two values that are contradictory. For example in the case of healthcare, the quality of service as value can be in conflict with privacy preservation. It is known that, having a personalised service that suits patients' expectations, the use of data listed as sensible are needed such as gender, age and others. If the team in charge of the project decides to prioritize quality service, there would definitely be a violation of privacy which is banned by AI ethics. Another conflict that can be observed is equality of the human right principle and equity in justice and fairness principle. This phenomenon is called **tensions** between values (Lo Piano 2020): It happens when two values witness points of friction. There are many ways to resolve those tensions as listed in Whittlestone et al. (2019). Overall, the process consists of measuring the importance of the values with respect to the society and then finding a trade-off between the two values.

1.2 Ethical Challenges in Existing in Domains

AI systems have shown great impact in different domains from health to education. Due to its enormous potential, AI has generated wide interest in the research community and industry as a whole. However, as these systems are being adopted by various institutions to make autonomous decisions on issues such as loan approvals, pretrial risk assessment etc., how do we ensure that the systems that are developed are not biased? What are the moral or ethical implications/challenges that would arise from these systems? In this subsection, we discuss the ethical challenges that are likely to exist in the use of autonomous systems in domains particularly relevant to African societies using agriculture and health domains as case studies.

Agriculture is one of the major sectors that serve as a means of livelihood for the majority of Africans with over 80% of the total urban food sales supplied by Africans (Africa Agriculture Status Report 2020). The Africa agriculture status report 2020 also projects African urbanization as one of the highest in the world. With the world's population expected to exceed 9 billion by 2050, this, therefore, would mean that the agricultural sector would need to increase its production levels up to about 70% (Kamilaris et al. 2017; Schönfeld et al. 2018) to be able to feed the world. The agriculture sector, therefore, needs to begin creating measures and possible solutions on how to increase food production. AI has been identified as one of the major solutions to this problem (Kumari et al. 2016; O'Grady and O'Hare 2017). AI can learn from historical data and learn patterns in the data to make predictions in the future. This ability of AI systems, therefore, makes it possible to be adopted by agricultural farmers to increase crop yield, identify crop disease, determine soil fertility and water levels.

AI systems however, learn well when presented with large amounts of data. The ethical challenge with working data is how to effectively measure if the data alone can capture all relevant information to correctly model the real-life experience, or if there is bias in the data. Does high accuracy from these models automatically translate to an efficient model which would also be accurate in practice? If these curated data are not accurate, they turn to translate to the developed autonomous systems. The efficiency of these autonomous systems could further lead to low yields, poor plant nutrition, and ill livestock, etc. Aside from the possibility of inaccurate data, there is the possibility of errors with the retrieval of data due to environmental circumstances. Most of the agriculture data are gathered through the use of sensors. However, farm animals can interfere with sensor equipment which would therefore lead to false readings (O'Grady and O'Hare 2017).

Furthermore, there are high development costs in building autonomous systems, which forces developers of these systems to sell them at exorbitant prices to cover production costs. Unfortunately, smallholder farmers, who should greatly benefit from these systems, cannot afford them. As such, how should AI systems developed with data from large-scale production farmers be used by a smallholder farmer whose data had no representations in the curated data training phase? Will such AI systems take into account such farmers' representations and characteristics? Will these systems not end up making biased decisions in favor of these farmer groups?

Health is another domain presented with a lot of ethical challenges when it comes to the deployment of AI in health systems. Many researchers have already pointed out how AI would revolutionize healthcare systems in the world, from the early detection of disease to drug development and clinical trials. Despite the potential benefits AI presents in this sector, we are also faced with the issue of data privacy and confidentiality. How will AI researchers developing systems ensure that individual data rights are protected? AI developed systems should provide ways in which data is protected as indicated by the National Institute of Health (NIH) Data Sharing policy and Implementation Guidelines which mentions that data needs to be widely and freely available, nevertheless it should protect the privacy and confidentiality of the data and individuals involved.

Moreover, a serious ethical challenge will be to deal with how to model fairness to avoid any form of bias. AI engineers/developers should be able to explain how an AI system made some decisions and why that particular decision was made. This would make it easier to interpret and explain these developed systems. In light of the recent COVID-19 pandemic, development has been made in the use of AI to reduce the negative impact of the pandemic on many nations. AI for instance was used to raise early warning towards the outbreak of the COVID-19 pandemic days before it was reported by international organizations. The haste in which emerging technologies are implemented and deployed, however, presents difficult ethical concerns and risks. The phenomenon of privacy issues over data collection, processing and analysis are becoming more pervasive and we need to place a closer emphasis on it (AI, Robots, and Ethics in the Age of COVID-19). Recently, in helping curb the exponential spread of the virus, most companies have put in place phone-based applications that seek to monitor people, self-diagnose oneself for COVID-19, contact tracing for people who may have come in contact with an infected person etc. However, who gets access to this vast amount of data that is generated? How long is the data going to be kept? What occurs when members of the public request that their data be returned?

The use of AI will not only present ethical challenges in agriculture and the health sector, the educational sector is also another domain that could be faced with serious ethical challenges. AI is currently being used to grade students, suggesting topics students need to spend considerable amounts of time to improve their grades etc.

1.3 Data Bias

One of the purposes of considering ethical principles in the design of artificial intelligences is to reduce the biases that may be consciously or unconsciously included during any stage of the design process. It is therefore important that learners know what these biases exist and how to mitigate its negative impact. Bias in AI can be defined as a phenomenon that occurs when a system's output is systematically prejudiced due to assumptions during the system development process (Mehrabi et al. 2019). There are basically two types of bias: Societal bias (or cognitive biases that are effective feelings towards a person or a group based on their perceived group membership) and data bias which is the lack of complete data of the case study (Mehrabi et al. 2019; Ntoutsi et al. 2020). This section focuses on data bias as it seems to be the one that is objective (not subjective compared to societal bias). In addition, data is to AI what blood is for human beings. In other words, without good data there is no hope for good results. As mentioned earlier, data bias is due to the use of data that is not well representative of the current situation.

According to (Aysolmaz et al. (2020), there are six types of biases: Sample or **Selected** bias, **Exclusion** bias, **Measurement** bias or **Systematic value distortion**, **Observer** or **Confirmation** bias, **Racial** bias, **Association or Stereotype** bias. The next paragraph will discuss each type by giving the definition, where it is inserted consciously or not in the development pipeline of the system.

Sample or **Selected** bias is when the dataset does not reflect the realities of the environment. This type of bias occurs mostly in the data collection process. **Exclusion** bias is when some features are categorised as non important and are removed. It's likely to happen during the feature engineering phase. **Measurement** bias or **systematic value distortion** is when the data used for training differs from the real world data or when faulty measurements result in data deformation. The stages concerned in the development are data collection. **Observer** or **Confirmation** bias is the way of seeing from data what is expected (assumptions) or wanted instead of truly paying attention to the output of the model. It happens when the team or developer goes into a project with subjective thoughts and is just looking for a confirmation of them. This bias is inserted during data labeling as well as in the training phase. **Racial** bias occurs when data skews in favor of particular demographics (gender, location, race, age). It is likely to be inserted during the data collection. **Association or Stereotype** bias happens when the data reinforces cultural bias. The consequences of data bias in Artificial Intelligence are very huge. They may lead to unfair systems, discriminatory outcomes, low accuracy models as well as analytical errors. To eliminate as much as possible, in 2016 the FAIR Guiding principles for scientific data management and stewardship were published in Scientific Data (FAIR Principles n.d.). The next paragraph will give details about the FAIR principles and explain how they are used to mitigate some biases listed above to reinforce Ethics AI principles.

FAIR stands for **F**indable **A**ccessible **I**nteroperable **R**eusable. It is a set of principles that aims to solve most of the issues in data management that reinforce data bias. FAIR principles set four characteristics that should have datasets for AI based solutions: findability, accessibility, interoperability and reusability. **Findability** is the way of assigning to datasets a globally unique identifier and enriching them with a lot of Metadata that can be indexed in a searchable resource for further use. This characteristic is crucial to mitigate data bias as it contributes to having datasets that contain a lot of information about specific subject matter which is good for AI systems as discussed in the previous section. This characteristic alone is suitable to reduce selection, exclusion, racial and stereotype biases. **Accessibility** is the way of giving people the right to know who is using their data as well as why and how their data are used through authentication and authorization systems. This feature is necessary to guarantee security, privacy and avoid data collection without the consent of people. **Interoperability** and **Reusability** characteristics ensure that the dataset can be linked with other applications for analysis and are sustainable.

1.4 Current State of Teaching AI Ethics

AI has been identified as having a great potential to further enhance developmental exploits throughout the African continent. A number of countries are championing these efforts by supporting and setting up hubs for further research and promotion of AI in many economic sectors. By 2035, the rate of growth of a country's GDP will be doubled by AI (Accenture-AI-Economic-Growth-Infographic) and several African governments believe that AI can serve as a solution to many countries' prevalent problems; from poverty reduction to easier delivery of healthcare and better education (Microsoft Corporation and Microsoft Corporation—2018—The Future Computed Artificial Intelligence and i.Pdf n.d.).

Thus, there have been initiatives such as the African AI accelerator, as well as global giants like Google setting up its first AI research and development center in Accra, Ghana (Google AI in Ghana 2018). University of Lagos launched the very first AI hub in Nigeria in 2018 with a focus on developing interests in AI among the youth (Data Science Nigeria Opens 1st Artificial Intelligence Hub in Unilag | The Guardian Nigeria News—Nigeria and World NewsTechnology—The Guardian Nigeria News—Nigeria and World News n.d.). Academic City University in Accra Ghana introduced the first undergraduate degree in Artificial Intelligence in Ghana. Other examples include Data Science Nigeria, and the IndabaX (IndabaX—Deep Learning Indaba 2021 n.d.), a program with the objective of encouraging conversations in machine learning and AI locally. IndabaX started in 2018 and currently boasts a membership of 27 countries across the continent. In April 2021, Nvidia's annual GTC (GTC 2021 n.d.) conference on breakthroughs in AI featured several African startups that presented innovative solutions that sought to tackle issues in agriculture, education, and healthcare and fintech in their respective countries. For example Dr CADx is a startup from Zimbabwe that has developed an AI-powered computer-aided diagnosis system to help doctors in the absence of radiologists. Their system can currently detect 15 pathologies in x-rays including Covid-19. Another startup presented a system for increasing access to clean energy in Africa through A.I.

Despite these efforts and gains in promoting the development of AI in Africa, the gap between AI development in Africa and the rest of the world is still very wide with countries like Mauritius, Egypt, South Africa, Kenya, Ghana, Namibia, Senegal and Morocco being the only countries in the top 100 on the 2020 *Global Government AI Readiness Index*. This report draws on 33 indicators across 10 different dimensions which include data availability, infrastructure, governance and ethics, vision, data representativeness, adaptability, digital capacity, human capital, size and innovation capacity (Table 1) to determine how ready a given government is to implement AI in the delivery of public services to their citizens.

The major indicators under the governance and ethics dimension included data protection and privacy legislation, cybersecurity, existence of a national ethics framework, legal framework's adaptability to digital business models. Under this dimension, it is observed that the score across all the African countries is still quite poor. Mauritius which ranks top on the continent only has a score of 58.34 compared to the number one (1) country, USA which has a score of 92.66.

The 2020 AI Readiness Index also introduced an assessment known as the Responsible AI Sub-index. This measures how responsibly governments make use of A.I by measuring 9 indicators across four (4) dimensions; Inclusivity, Accountability, Transparency and Privacy. It is interesting to note that countries like Senegal and Mauritius ranked 9th and 13th respectively while the U.S.A (number 1 on the Readiness Index) ranked lower at 24th. Similarly, Estonia, which is 17th on the AI Global Readiness

Table 1 Sample of scores of the A.I readiness index comparing U.S.A (ranked 1st) to the African countries listed in the top 100

Country	Infrastructure	Data representativeness	Data availability	Governance and ethics	Digital capacity	Rank
USA	90.41	89.16	89.55	92.66	88.83	1
Mauritius	47.80	73.36	63.70	58.34	53.51	45
Egypt	37.39	48.90	59.49	56.50	48.61	56
South Africa	74.84	74.24	67.56	51.91	50.59	58
Kenya	41.29	64.13	47.32	44.52	65.43	71
Rwanda	36.43	52.09	44.29	57.91	76.11	87
Ghana	37.52	70.75	57.95	48.24	51.72	91
Namibia	42.73	71.67	48.87	38.62	41.58	96
Senegal	38.05	63.49	50.61	44.75	47.98	97
Morocco	45.53	31.64	62.15	46.31	47.07	99

Index, was 1st on the responsible A.I sub-index list. This trend indicates that the countries positioned at the highest rank of AI readiness are not necessarily higher in their practice of responsible AI. The 2020 responsible A.I sub-index covered only 34 countries and 4 countries out of these were from the African continent. However, this presents an opportunity for other countries to develop strategies to ensure that while they take advantage of the positive impacts of A.I for development, policies can also be put in place to promote ethical uses of A.I. especially at the government level.

Education is one the most important mechanisms for pushing the awareness of AI ethics. The past decade has seen many top universities and research institutions, such as the University of Nairobi, Ghana, or Cairo, introduce AI as courses in their computing and engineering departments. Most of these educational institutions, however, do not currently have AI ethics as part of their syllabi. A few of them, such as the University of Botswana, have a separate course known as Social Informatics which focuses on ethical, social, legal issues in computer science. In another example, the Centre for A.I research (CAIR) Ethics of AI research group at the University of Pretoria focuses on teaching and research on machine ethics, the ethics of social robotics, neuro-ethics and data ethics.

But these examples are still too few and far between. With AI steadily gaining visibility in academia and research institutions across Africa, it is necessary to further encourage learners and future developers in particular to understand the ethical issues involved in the design, development and use of AI applications though the discussion of these issue in higher education.

1.5 Best Approaches to Teaching AI Ethics

In 2002, Pratt (2002) proposed five approaches to teaching usually used in secondary and higher education. In this section, we discuss each of them and tell how they can be relevant to teaching AI ethics. **The transmission perspective** refers to the transfer from teacher to learners, a specific body of the knowledge through a structured lecture and includes seminar format and conferences. This perspective can be useful for teaching ethical design of algorithms or teaching decision making methodologies.

The **developmental approach** which aims to propose grows the mindset of the learner. It might change the mindset of the learner if the content delivered is not in line with their understanding. It might strengthen the mindset of the learner if the content is in line with theirs. It works with questioning and examples that make the learner think out of the box. Furey and Martin (2019) used this approach to raise ethical thinking about autonomous vehicles. This form of teaching is also suitable for research students. It helps to cultivate critical thinking and ethical reasoning skills, which are highly relevant in AI development and ethics (Borenstein and Howard 2021), to set or understand ethical principles and values as well as codes of conduct (Wilk n.d.). It can be done through both seminars and discussions formats. For instance, organising a series of talks on a specific topic of AI ethics and giving the opportunity to many teachers to share their opinion with respect to their background and interact with the learners.

The **Apprenticeship Approach** aims to challenge the learners with the real environment as an internship. In that context, learning occurs when the students start to adopt the language, values, and practices of the specific activity. This form can be reserved for students in the specialisation phase: Ethics AI in Education, Ethics AI in Agriculture, Ethics AI in Computer vision etc.... This pipeline is suitable to increase student's familiarity with professional code of ethics as well as balancing theory and practice of AI ethics. It can be made by using world datasets that require students to address ethical issues in AI.

From the **Nurturing Approach**, the goal of teaching is to give enough support (care) to the learners in order to build their confidence in order to have an impact on their competence. It is suitable for elementary education (primary schools). In essence, there is no one approach to it, learners should be allowed to think and learn on their own and grow as individuals. Teachers should support students and not impose on learners what they as teachers necessarily deem right.

Finally, the **Social Reform Perspective** aims to bring about social change, not simply individual learning. Learners are called to take social actions for better conditions in their environments. Activities involved in this type of teaching are bringing learners in diverse communities, encouraging learners to take a critical stance, watching documentaries and discussing. For instance, the documentary (Coded Bias) is a great resource to point out algorithmic bias in AI systems.

Overall, the best approach for teaching AI ethics is the mix of all the approaches listed above with respect to the type of learners and the expectations of the lesson.

For a specific case of higher education, the combination of transmission, developmental and apprenticeship might be the best approaches regarding their goals and the activities included. In addition, there are some practices that should be essential to reinforce AI Ethics skills to future AI leaders in Africa including creating diverse working AI groups composed from both technical and non technical people. Diversity is essential for ethics in general.

1.6 Goal (Where Do We Need to Be with Teaching AI Ethics)

The need for teaching AI ethics cannot be overstated and all indications have shown the necessity of this. For instance, Google has put together the nature of AI applications they would and would not pursue as their AI principles of which they are putting in practice (Google AI Our Principles n.d.). The launch of Montréal Declaration for a Responsible Development of Artificial Intelligence (Montréal Declaration) with its main focus to foster a responsible development of AI (Responsible AI Declaration 2018). Conferences such as ACM FaCCT also seek to bring in a diverse group of researchers and practitioners interested in the area of fairness and accountability to discuss and tackle emerging issues in this area. All of these initiatives seek to address the issue of teaching AI ethics to future developers and practitioners. But then, where exactly do we as Africans need to be as a continent with regards to teaching AI ethics?

First and foremost, teaching AI ethics and ensuring that all students take courses in AI ethics is not a debatable topic. As a matter of urgency, AI ethics should be a compulsory course for all students to take. As many industries continue to incorporate AI technologies into their operations, everyone at some point in time will come into contact with using AI developed applications, whether one is an AI software developer or not. It is therefore important that as we train the next future generation, they learn to pause and think about the ethical consequences of the technologies they come into contact with or while developing them. AI developers are often focused on having the performance of their models increase while paying little attention to the complex ethical considerations at play when designing AI systems. In view of this, future AI developers should be taught how to design AI systems for healthy outcomes devoid of any form of bias.

Second, we should be at a point where students have a fostering AI ethics mindset. While teaching AI ethics, student AI developers should be able to understand that the AI technologies they are developing are linked with ethical concerns and they have a paramount role to find ways to deal with these ethical issues. Most often, developers turn to look at AI ethics as another person's problem to deal with. However, in training AI technologies, the developer has a choice to decide which particular features should be useful in the model. Take for instance, an AI system that is able to classify transactions as fraudulent or non-fraudulent. The developer needs to decide how to choose/eliminate sensitive features like ethnicity, sex etc. to train the model to ensure that these systems do not carry any form of bias. As such, we need to be at the state where students have a fostering AI ethics mindset and not see studying ethics as the sole responsibility of a sub group of people interested in ethics.

Third, the understanding of ethical principles differ from person to person and place to place. As such in teaching AI ethics it is important to have a diverse team of instructors (from lawyers to philosophers etc.). This will give students different perspectives in understanding ethics and when developing or using AI technologies. We need to be at a state where teaching of AI ethics is of priority to everyone notwithstanding the background of the individual or organization involved.

Lastly, higher institutions should by now have instituted multiple ways to teach AI ethics to future generations. As there is no right or wrong answers to answering ethical questions, since these turn to differ from place to place. Teaching modes should incorporate discussions about the ethical problems and how to make ethical decisions. Seminars and papers presentation could also be fused in the mode of instructions. This gives students the liberty to think and write down their own ethical challenges and come up with suggested ways in handling them. Particularly, AI ethics classes should provide a complete blend of theory and practice. Case studies could be presented to students and allow them to ponder and deliberate over the ethical issues associated with these case studies and suggest ways of dealing with them.

As AI is becoming a massive technology impacting our lives, we need to direct its use in a more socially responsible manner and this needs to start early on in the training and education process. It is expected that as of now, students should have developed the fostering AI ethics mindset and always pause to think about the ethical concerns while developing AI technologies or before using them. But, how can they do this if it is not thoroughly incorporated into their learning? Higher education could start by making AI ethics a compulsory course for all students to take with additional multiple ways of imparting AI ethics training to younger ones as well using the approaches described above.

2 Conclusion

In the recent cases of ethical issues that cause harm to many end users in AI applications, most of the problems detected were due to the lack of consideration of some ethical principles during the lifecycle of development. While at the moment, Africa as a continent is not ranked at the top in terms of the development and use of AI, it is just a matter of time before the tables start turning. Africa has been identified as the continent for the next industrial revolution after Asia. Furthermore, AI is gradually becoming an integral part of industrial and economic advancements on the continent. Africa, therefore, needs to take advantage of AI in its developmental agenda. However, African countries should learn from others failures to produce better solutions that are ethically right. Therefore, the need to incorporate ethical values to AI systems is paramount. The first step to ensure it is by educating the future leaders of AI development in Africa about ethical principles and in order to make them fully understand the impact of these tools on society. African institutions can start by putting together educational policies where AI is a relevant field of study. This needs to be accompanied by teaching ethical issues related to AI development and usage.

Teaching ethics is easier when a general set of guidelines is written down for a group of people to follow rather than contextualizing it to what the specific individual or group of people perceive as right or wrong and good or bad. It is however recommended in this chapter that, in teaching AI ethics on the African continent, it is important to stress on certain key principles: respect of human rights, respect for society and the environment, robustness and safety, transparency, contestability, responsibility or accountability, justice and fairness, and privacy. It is also highlighted that these principles will go a long way to help in addressing challenges faced in societal domains like agriculture and healthcare and also find solutions to issues in data bias.

References

2019—Ethical and Societal Implications of Data and Arti.pdf. n.d. https://www.nuffieldfoundation.org/sites/default/files/files/Ethical-and-Societal-Implications-of-Data-and-AI-report-Nuffield-Foundat.pdf. Accessed 1 June 2021.
Accenture-AI-Economic-Growth-Infographic.pdf. n.d. https://www.accenture.com/_acnmedia/PDF-57/Accenture-AI-Economic-Growth-Infographic.pdf. Accessed 1 June 2021.
Africa Agriculture Status Report 2020—AGRA. n.d. https://agra.org/africa-agriculture-status-report-2020/. Accessed 1 June 2021.
AI+Readiness+Report.pdf. n.d. https://static1.squarespace.com/static/58b2e92c1e5b6c8280584 84e/t/5f7747f29ca3c20ecb598f7c/1601653137399/AI+Readiness+Report.pdf. Accessed 1 June 2021.
AI, Robots, and Ethics in the Age of COVID-19. n.d. https://sloanreview.mit.edu/article/ai-robots-and-ethics-in-the-age-of-covid-19/. Accessed 1 June 2021.
AIHLEG_EthicsGuidelinesforTrustworthyAI-ENpdf.pdf. n.d. https://ai.bsa.org/wp-content/uploads/2019/09/AIHLEG_EthicsGuidelinesforTrustworthyAI-ENpdf.pdf. Accessed 1 June 2021.
Aysolmaz, B., Dau, N., and Iren, D. (2020). *Preventing algorithmic bias in the development of algorithmic decision-making systems: A Delphi study*. Proceedings of the Annual Hawaii International Conference on
Borenstein, J., and A. Howard. 2021. Emerging Challenges in AI and the Need for AI Ethics Education. *AI and Ethics* 1 (1): 61–65. https://doi.org/10.1007/s43681-020-00002-7.
'Coded Bias' Is the Most Important Film About AI You Can Watch Today. n.d. https://www.vice.com/en/article/n7v8mx/coded-bias-netflix-documentary-ai-ethics-surveil. Accessed 4 June 2021.
Montréal Institute for Learning Algorithms. (2018). Montréal Declaration for a Responsible Development of Artificial Intelligence. 1-21. https://www.montrealdeclaration-responsibleai.com/
Department of Industry, S. 2019. *AI Ethics Principles* [Text]. Department of Industry, Science, Energy and Resources; Department of Industry, Science, Energy and Resources. https://www.industry.gov.au/data-and-publications/building-australias-artificial-intelligence-capability/ai-ethics-framework/ai-ethics-principles.
FAIR Principles. n.d. GO FAIR. https://www.go-fair.org/fair-principles/. Accessed 1 June 2021.
Furey, H., and F. Martin. 2019. AI Education Matters: A Modular Approach to AI Ethics Education. *AI Matters* 4(4): 13–15. https://doi.org/10.1145/3299758.3299764.

Google AI in Ghana. 2018. Google. https://blog.google/around-the-globe/google-africa/google-ai-ghana/

GTC 2021: #1 AI Conference. n.d. NVIDIA. https://www.nvidia.com/en-us/gtc/. Accessed 1 June 2021.

Herzfeld, N. 2002. Creating in Our Own Image: Artificial Intelligence and the Image of God. *Zygon®*, 37(2), 303–316. https://doi.org/10.1111/0591-2385.00430.

IndabaX—Deep Learning Indaba 2021. n.d. https://deeplearningindaba.com/2021/indabax/. Accessed 1 June 2021.

Kamilaris, A., A. Kartakoullis, and F.X. Prenafeta-Boldú. 2017. A Review on the Practice of Big Data Analysis in Agriculture. *Computers and Electronics in Agriculture* 143: 23–37. https://doi.org/10.1016/j.compag.2017.09.037.

Kumari, S.V., P. Bargavi, and U. Subhashini. 2016. Role of Big Data Analytics in Agriculture. *International Journal of Computing Science and Mathematics Engineering* 3: 110–113.

Leslie, D. 2019. Understanding Artificial Intelligence Ethics and Safety: A Guide for the Responsible Design and Implementation of AI Systems in the Public Sector. *Zenodo.* https://doi.org/10.5281/ZENODO.3240529.

Lo Piano, S. 2020. Ethical Principles in Machine Learning and Artificial Intelligence: Cases from the Field and Possible Ways Forward. *Humanities and Social Sciences Communications* 7 (1): 9. https://doi.org/10.1057/s41599-020-0501-9.

MBA, M.K.M., BSN, RN-BC, Director, N., Industry, U.P., Officer, C.N., & Microsoft. 2019. *Artificial Intelligence in Health: Ethical Considerations for Research and Practice | HIMSS.* https://www.himss.org/resources/artificial-intelligence-health-ethical-considerations-research-and-practice.

Mehrabi, N., F., Morstatter, N., Saxena, K., Lerman, and A. Galstyan. 2019. A Survey on Bias and Fairness in Machine Learning. http://arxiv.org/abs/1908.09635.

Ntoutsi, E., P. Fafalios, U. Gadiraju, V. Iosifidis, W. Nejdl, M.-E. Vidal, S. Ruggieri, F. Turini, S. Papadopoulos, E. Krasanakis, I. Kompatsiaris, K. Kinder-Kurlanda, C. Wagner, F. Karimi, M. Fernandez, H. Alani, B. Berendt, T. Kruegel, C. Heinze, et al. 2020. Bias in Data-Driven Artificial Intelligence Systems—An Introductory Survey. *Wires Data Mining and Knowledge Discovery* 10 (3): e1356. https://doi.org/10.1002/widm.1356.

O'Grady, M.J., and G.M.P. O'Hare. 2017. Modelling the smart farm. *Information Processing in Agriculture* 4 (3): 179–187. https://doi.org/10.1016/j.inpa.2017.05.001.

Pratt, D.D. 2002. Good Teaching: One Size Fits All? *New Directions for Adult and Continuing Education* 2002 (93): 5–16. https://doi.org/10.1002/ace.45.

Schönfeld, M.V., R., Heil, and L. Bittner. 2018. Big Data on a Farm—Smart Farming. In *Big Data in Context*, eds. T. Hoeren, and B. Kolany-Raiser, 109–120. Springer International Publishing. https://doi.org/10.1007/978-3-319-62461-7_12.

Stahl, B.C. 2021. Artificial Intelligence for a Better Future: An Ecosystem Perspective on the Ethics of AI and Emerging Digital Technologies. *Springer International Publishing.* https://doi.org/10.1007/978-3-030-69978-9.

Uni_ethical_ai.pdf. n.d. http://www.thefutureworldofwork.org/media/35420/uni_ethical_ai.pdf. Accessed 1 June 2021.

Whittlestone, J., R., Nyrup, A., Alexandrova, and S., Cave. 2019. The Role and Limits of Principles in AI Ethics: Towards a Focus on Tensions. In *Proceedings of the 2019 AAAI/ACM Conference on AI, Ethics, and Society*, 195–200. https://doi.org/10.1145/3306618.3314289.

Open Access This chapter is licensed under the terms of the Creative Commons Attribution 4.0 International License (http://creativecommons.org/licenses/by/4.0/), which permits use, sharing, adaptation, distribution and reproduction in any medium or format, as long as you give appropriate credit to the original author(s) and the source, provide a link to the Creative Commons license and indicate if changes were made.

The images or other third party material in this chapter are included in the chapter's Creative Commons license, unless indicated otherwise in a credit line to the material. If material is not included in the chapter's Creative Commons license and your intended use is not permitted by statutory regulation or exceeds the permitted use, you will need to obtain permission directly from the copyright holder.

The manufacturer's authorised representative in the EU is Springer Nature Customer Service Centre GmbH, Europaplatz 3, 69115 Heidelberg, Germany. If you have any concerns regarding our products, please contact ProductSafety@springernature.com

Printed and bound by CPI Group (UK) Ltd, Croydon, CR0 4YY

23/03/2026

02076360-0007